I0839996

Power and Pretense

© 2018

P.S. Winn

**This book is a work of fiction.
The names, places, characters and
happenings are a work of the author's
imagination. Any resemblance to people,
places or actual happenings is purely
coincidental.**

This book and the others by P.S. Winn
are available on Amazon books

http://www.amazon.com/author/pswinn

Also on Barnes and Noble
www.barnesandnoble.com/c/p.s.-winn

A journey is best when shared with others.

Let the journey begin.

P.S. Winn

Chapter 1

Walking through the FBI building, Brock Odom was waiting for someone to pull a joke on him. Being April fool's day, Brock was surprised that one of his fellow agents hadn't come up with a stupid joke yet. He could remember many years in the past finding himself the brunt of many April fool's tricks. Maybe that's why when he received the request to head to Aaron Jackson's office, Brock hadn't worried. A grin played around his mouth and the green eyes sparkled, wondering what foolish thing was coming.

Knocking on the door, Brock waited until he heard the gruff sound of his boss yelling 'come on in', before he slowly pushed open the door.

One step inside and Brock knew the request wasn't a joke and something was wrong. Aaron Jackson wasn't a man who got upset easily. Today, the man who usually was relaxed and the picture of composure, was anything but. The white hair looked like a hand had run through more than once causing the hair to stand up in disarray on Aaron's head.

Sitting behind his desk, Aaron motioned a hand over the top of his desk, littered with papers, and nodded at Brock.

"Take a seat Agent Odom, but close that door behind you first. We have a new case."

Brock shook his head of thick, dark hair and shut the door. "I'm already working a case. You know that Aaron. Hell, we're really getting close to solving the robberies. In fact, we're only a few days away from grabbing one of the bank executives. Maybe even a couple. The robberies are definitely an inside job."

As Brock sat down, Aaron threw a yellow eight by ten envelope over the desk toward him. The daunting, intense blue eyes held a hard stare. "Sorry Brock. That case can be handled by the others. I want you on this one."

Brock frowned as he pulled the envelope toward him and then stared down at it. The first thing he noticed was the lack of a return address. He turned the large envelope over to look at the blank back side before flipping it back to the front. Besides the FBI address, Brock only saw the postmark showing the origination was Montana.

Brock sighed, he was from the state, but never had the time, nor the inclination lately to go back. Brock slowly opened the large envelope and pulled out several papers stapled together. The first page was a cover sheet. The only writing on the paper was the word Reparation in bold letters. With a frown etching lines in his forehead, Brock turned to the second page and began reading.

The green eyes widened and then narrowed as Brock scanned down the page. He didn't take time to read each item thoroughly, but the gist of the pages had him looking up and staring at his boss. He shook his head. "This can't be legit. What is this an April fool's joke or something?"

Seeing the serious look in the blue eyes across from him, Brock sighed. "Are you really taking this thing seriously?"

Aaron nodded, face grim. "We sure in the hell are. I've already arranged for agents to set up camp at each of the locations listed in the threats."

Brock frowned. "So, why am I here? Like I said I'm really knee deep in the robbery investigation. On top of that, you must know I'm about the worst agent you could bring in. You know how I feel about the President. Hell, you know how he degrades all of the intelligence agencies. He wants to see us discredited and even shut down."

Aaron grinned slightly. "First off, I should say I'm sorry. I forgot it was April first. Second, I think you are the perfect agent. Did you notice the last location and the postmark on the list? You were born and bred in Montana. What can you tell me about Deer Valley?"

Brock grunted. "From what I remember, every damn valley in Montana was packed with deer. For all I know they were all called Deer Valley. What does that have to do with you calling me in here today? The last location on that list said something about the President's newest property. I didn't know he had a place in Montana and why would he choose a place called Deer Valley anyway? From experience, we both know the man is all about flashy places and photo-ops."

Nodding, Aaron sighed. "The President purchased a hotel in the Montana Capital of Helena, not in Deer Valley. If you look closer at the postmark, the letter was mailed from Deer Valley, Montana. We also have acquired the video of the man who mailed the letter from that location. We're sure he didn't write the letter. Your first job is to go talk to the guy. You need to lean on him and get some answers. I'm going to send agent Mackey with you to get that done."

The green eyes staring at Aaron turned down in a curious frown. "Kim Mackey?"

Aaron nodded and laughed. "I thought a little feminine persuasion might be helpful. She's more than qualified for the job."

Brock nodded. "Damn straight, from what I've heard about Kim, I'd trust her with my life. I was just surprised. We've never worked together before. You know James Long is my partner."

Aaron shrugged. "He's also the other person who knows the most about the robberies you were working on. That's why I'm keeping him on that case."

Brock looked back down at the pages and frowned as he read the beginning lines out loud.

"This is not a hoax. I am a law abiding conservative American. I can no longer let our Government ruin America. Payback in the form of a reparation to fix the wrong doings begins on the third day of April. If no one will stand up against the degradation the President has forced on this country, I have no choice but to take matters into my own hands."

Lifting his head, Brock stared wide eyed at Aaron. "The third is only two days away."

The sound of Aaron's deep sigh filled his office. "The letter says a bomb will explode every day from the third until the big finale in Montana on the ninth."

Aaron shook his head. "By the way, the

President has a ribbon cutting ceremony scheduled in his hotel in Montana on that same day. Some place he calls Treasure Hill Resort."

Running a hand through his dark hair, Brock echoed Aaron's sigh. "I'm guessing since the man who mailed this damn thing isn't your suspect, you've already dug up some background on him."

Aaron nodded. "All the information is in a neat little package prepared especially for you and agent Mackey. I thought you could go over it on the plane. It will be a great way for the two of you to pass the time. I'm told, even without layovers, you're in for over five hours in the air. You'll land in the capital, grab a rental car and head to Deer Valley. We were lucky the place had a motel and I got both of you reservations."

The green eyes stared at Aaron in disbelief as Brock shook his head. "I know you think you have me pegged as the perfect guy for this assignment, but I haven't stepped foot in Montana since I graduated high school. No one in my family even lives there anymore." Brock grunted. "I'll gladly take the assignment. I just don't want you getting the impression I'm some kind of hometown hero. No one will bend over backwards to turn over evidence to me."

Aaron laughed. "The thought never crossed my mind. But, you lived in the country. Hell, I've seen your place, you live way out in the middle of nowhere. Maybe that will give you an edge. Even without that, the fact is, you're a damn good agent. That's why I made my decision. I've got agents checking into the locations on the list. Universal Access studio is the first target. The letter says the bomber picked that place because they only released the one tape of the President's abusive boasting. Apparently this guy feels like the Universal Access Company has more they are just sitting on." Aaron grunted. "Not that it would matter, after the first one got all the air time, it didn't make a difference. I'm hoping if we stop that bombing, this maniac will think twice about the others scheduled."
Aaron looked at his watch. "I'm sorry for the short notice. Your plane leaves in four hours. Agent Mackey is also being briefed. Another agent will be picking her up from

her apartment and then swinging by your house to grab you."

Watching Aaron stand up, Brock echoed the motion and got to his feet. He shook the hand offered by Aaron. "Although I'm the last one standing in line to help the fanatic sitting in the oval office, I'll do whatever I can to stop the other, equally demented, man."

Releasing Brock's hand, Aaron placed a hand on the agent's shoulder. "Just don't tell anyone else about your feelings about the President. He'd use anything to discredit us. The jerk doesn't realize we're protecting him. I never doubted your loyalty to the job or to the country."

Brock frowned. "Have you notified the Secret Service and the President?"

Aaron shrugged. "I talked to the Secret Service agents. I'll leave it up to them to decide what they want to share with the President. With his paranoid spiel, it might be better if they kept this from him. I'm not worried about him. The bombings are set up in places where too many innocent people could get killed and for the wrong reasons. I just want you to worry about squeezing the mailer of the letter for information. I'll maintain close contact with both you and Agent Mackey to keep you in the loop on the other threats."

Aaron smiled. "Now get the hell out of here. I want you to be ready to catch that plane."

Brock grinned. "Don't worry, I'll be on it. Like you said, it's not the President, but the other people I'm worried about protecting. I hate to say it, but the author of the letter has a damn good point. Someone should have had the backbone to remove the President from office a long time ago. It's a shame to think a person decided it will take the committing of atrocities to accomplish that."

Nodding, Aaron moved to the door. "Just remember what I said about keeping those thoughts to yourself. The President would love to have information that proves we are biased so he can discredit us."

Aaron shrugged. "Who knows, maybe we can stop these bombings and gain back some of the credibility and respect the President stripped away."

Brock nodded at the statement even though he didn't believe what Aaron was hoping for was actually feasible. The President had a following, although small, that for some reason was preventing many in congress from standing up against the man. Brock couldn't remember a time when putting politics over people had been more prevalent.

Chapter 2

Leaving the FBI headquarters, Brock got in his sixty five mustang and headed for home. Aaron had been right, although Brock only lived twenty minutes from the city, his home felt like it was a world away.
The five acres his house sat on looked like they belonged more to the state he would be heading toward instead of the city he had just left.

Pulling his car into his garage, Brock hoped the trip to Montana wouldn't end up being an extended stay. He employed one hired hand to maintain his property, but liked to be close enough to keep an eye on things. Luke Sparrow, who also had a small house on Brock's land was a good person and hard worker. Brock paid the man not only a wage, but included the home in Luke's salary. Brock didn't mind the extra benefit because, as an FBI agent, he was away from home regrettably more days than he was present. Thinking about that, Brock added calling Luke and explaining, to his mental list of things to do.

Stepping in his house, Brock headed to his bedroom. Pulling out his well-used duffle bag, Brock threw in a weeks' worth of clothes. Having grown up in Montana and remembering the uncertainty of the weather, Brock added long sleeve shirts and a couple light jackets to the collection. In DC, the temperatures had been running in the seventies. Brock had seen many Aprils growing up when several inches of snow had covered the Montana landscape.

After packing, Brock headed to the kitchen to grab a sandwich. Aaron hadn't said which of the many planes the FBI had access to would be carrying both him and agent Mackey to Montana. Past experience told Brock dinner seldom came as normal operating procedure. That in mind, he sat down at the table and ate his sandwich. He wished he would have gotten Kim's number from Aaron. Because she wasn't an agent he would normally work with, Brock had no idea how to reach her. From what he had heard, Kim had a good reputation with the department. He had seen her at conferences and award ceremonies where both of them had been given separate accolades. Despite Kim's recognitions for her service, Brock knew nothing about her personal life. Brock grinned, knowing he was about to find out a lot about Kim in the days to come and vice versa. The one thing about working with a new partner was finding out quickly if the two of you were compatible. Brock had been lucky in the seven years he'd been an agent. He could only remember one time when he had been unable to get along with an agent he worked with. Apparently he wasn't alone in his feelings, the man was serving time in federal prison for abusing more than one subject he'd taken into custody.

Brock shook bad memories from his head and took the time he had left to give Luke a call. After explaining to his employee that he'd be out of town for an uncertain amount of time, Brock hung up, satisfied Luke would handle everything. A task he'd been given several times in the past.

Leaving the kitchen, Brock headed back to the bedroom to grab his bag and shoulder holster. He added a Kevlar vest to the bag. The FBI issued vest was something Brock kept close, when he wasn't wearing it. Years at the FBI had Brock feeling naked without his Glock and his vest.

Ten minutes later, Brock heard the sound of a vehicle pulling into his driveway. Grabbing his bag, and slipping on his shoulder holster, Brock locked up as he stepped out of his house. Looking at the plain, black SUV, Brock grinned and shook his head. The agency liked non-descript vehicles, but Brock would take his red sixty five mustang over one of the drab vehicles any day.

The passenger door of the SUV opened and a man vaguely familiar to Brock, stepped out. "Agent Odom, if you'd like to throw your bag in the back, we can be on our way."

Doing as he was told, Brock let the man open the back door for him before sliding into the backseat where Kim Mackey was already waiting.

Brock smiled at her. "Agent Mackey, I'm Brock Odom. I know we've never worked together before, but I'm damn glad Aaron partnered me up with someone with such a good reputation."

The brown eyes staring at Brock were half hidden by long, dark blonde bangs. The eyes narrowed a bit as Kim considered Brock's words. Deciding he was sincere, she smiled. "Thanks Brock, I've heard a lot of good things about you also. Since we're going to be spending time together, I'm Kim, not agent Mackey."

Nodding, Brock put out his hand. When Kim shook it, Brock's green eyes lit up. "I just hope Deer Valley isn't as boring as it sounds. Born and raised in Montana, I know a lot of towns have under five hundred people."

Kim laughed. "Hell, that should make finding the perp a lot easier."

Brock nodded, but knew finding the guy was only step one in their job. Getting him to talk was something totally different.

The two agents sat back in their seats as the SUV headed away from Brock's house. As they drove past the wooden fence that surrounded his property, Kim shook her head. "I can't believe you live here. I've always lived in a big, crowded city. All this open area would take some getting used to."

Brock laughed. "I like it. After the time I spend in the city, it's relaxing."

Kim nodded although she didn't quite agree with Brock's statement.

The two were quiet for the short time it took to arrive at the airport. Pulling in, the agents saw not only a plane waiting for them, but were surprised to see Aaron standing on the tarmac. Brock turned to Kim.
"Looks like the boss is already keeping an eye on us."

Looking out through Brock's window, Kim nodded. "Maybe he wants to join us in Montana."

The two got out of the vehicle and retrieved their bags from the back before heading over to Aaron.

He was holding up two file folders.

"I brought you the information you'll need. I could have had them delivered to the plane, but decided I needed a break from the office and brought them out myself."

Handing one file to Kim and the other to Brock, Aaron's blue eyes turned serious.

"Inside you will find extra information on not only Cory Baxter, the mailer of the bomb threats, but on Sheriff Walt Danvers. He's in charge in Deer Valley and I believe he is probably the man who knows Cory Baxter better than anyone else. I also wanted to tell you both good luck. I believe we have the agents who can find the bombs and dismantle them, but I want the guy behind the threats. I'm hoping this guy in Deer Valley will hand him over to you."

Both agents nodded, knowing the agencies reputation was on the line. It had been the President, who was also a target, who had degraded all intelligence agencies even before he had unexpectantly won the election.

Not wanting to think about any of that, let alone talk about it, Brock pointed at the

plane, hoping to avoid the subject.
"I'm glad you reserved us seats on one of
the deluxe models for the long flight."

Aaron laughed. "Only the best. Hey, you're
both damn lucky. I could tell you horror
stories about a few of the planes I've had to
catch flights on."

Kim laughed lightly. "I really appreciate it.
I've been on a few of the no frills flights
myself."

Rubbing his hands together while glancing
at his watch, Aaron sighed. "Time for me to
get back and for you two to head out. Keep
in touch, I want updates on anything and
everything. Believe me, every small detail is
needed on this one."

With guarantees to keep close contact, Kim
and Brock watched Aaron leave before they
boarded the plane.

Brock and Kim were escorted past several
passengers, who both knew were fellow
agents, to a closed off area that held four
chairs and a table. The furnishings looked
like they would fit easily into a home owned

by someone with an income higher than either of the agents made.

After the two stashed their bags in the overhead compartments, they were offered soft drinks. The two settled into their seats, but waited until the woman returned with their drinks and then left them alone, before placing their folders on the table.

As each started reading the material in front of them, Kim frowned. Lowering her papers, she stared at Brock. The brown eyes narrowed. "The first location along with the explanation for the bomb threat doesn't make sense to me."

Placing a finger on the page he'd been reading, Brock looked across at Kim. "I haven't thoroughly read through the threats. I skimmed that part of the papers in Aaron's office. I was more interested in the perp who did the mailing."

With a sigh, Kim brushed the blonde bangs away from her eyes. Although her hair was cut short, the front was a bit longer. Kim felt like she was always making the motion, but liked the hair style despite the fact.

"According to this letter, the bomber is sure the Universal Access studios have more video footage that shows the President's immoral acts. The problem is, this guy, if the perp is a male, isn't threatening the studio if they don't release the material. Wouldn't you think that would be the number one demand before someone used the threat of bombing to get what they wanted?"

Hesitating a moment, Brock thought about the question, then shrugged. "Maybe not, think about everything the President has done. It seems like nothing sticks to that guy. Hell, the bomber probably figured the big wigs at Universal Access were bought off a long time ago. If there are more videos, they have long since been destroyed. Or maybe they are archived in the President's private studio. I also know the agents Aaron put in charge won't leave a stone unturned. They may be getting into that place to stop a bombing, but once inside, they'll have to do a thorough search for not only the bomb, but any other threats. If other evidence is uncovered, even if it insinuates the President, it will have to be preserved."

Brock grinned. "Right now, our headache is talking to Cory Baxter in Deer Valley." Brock held up the pages he'd been reading. "The last two pages in your folder are his profile. From the looks of it, Mr. Baxter is well known to the law in Deer Valley."

Letting out a sigh, Kim nodded. She still felt like something didn't add up about the first threat, but Brock was right, they had a job to do. Just like the other agents had their assignments to complete. She flipped to the last pages and began reading. The more they knew about Cory Baxter, the easier it would be to find what they needed to make him talk.

Kim read the physical profile out loud. "Cory Baxter, no middle name. Age twenty three, height five foot ten, weight one hundred and fifty pounds. Auburn hair, green eyes."

Across from Kim, Brock grunted. "The guy could blow away in a strong wind."

Smiling at Brock, Kim nodded. "He doesn't even outweigh me by much and he's a half a foot taller."

Looking back at the page, Kim continued reading. "Parents deceased, no siblings. Tattoo of the name Cory on the left shoulder and a small tiger on his chest."
Kim frowned. "I imagine those are jailhouse tattoos. Looks like our new friend Cory Baxter has spent more than a few days incarcerated."

Brock nodded. "That's true, but most are petty offenses. Looks like this guy likes to drink and then get abusive."

Kim nodded, knowing a lot of people with similar traits. "My husband is a cop. He sees more of that than he cares too."

The green eyes opened wide. "Hell, I didn't even know you were married. How does the hubby feel about you flying off to wilds of Montana with a great catch like me?"

Kim smiled. "Sorry Brock, the husband is a bigger catch and he knows it. Blake knows what my job is like and all that entails. We were married six months before I officially became an agent. Four and a half years since we got married and no complaints. With his being a cop, and a damn good one, I think

his understanding is on a higher level than some. Blake is a big guy with dark hair and eyes that stands out in a crowd."
Kim laughed. "Especially when he is standing next to me. I'm about as light as Blake is dark."
Shrugging, Kim frowned. "What about you? Do you have a wife or kids? I don't know anything about your personal life."

Brock laughed because he had been thinking the same thing about Kim earlier.
He shook his head. "No wife, no kids and no time to worry about it. You have a husband, what about kids?"

Kim shook her head. "No kids. Like you said, no time. I find being married and an agent more than enough excitement in my life for now."

Forgetting about the papers they had been reading, the two took time to get to know each other while the plane flew from one end of the country almost to the other. Neither realizing how much time was passing until they heard the overhead announcement to prepare for landing.
The two agents slipped the essential folders

into the luggage they pulled from the overhead compartments, before sitting down and buckling up as the plane descended.

After landing, Kim and Brock walked out of the compartment to prepare for unloading. Both were surprised at first to see several others from the plane joining them. Although the two nodded and smiled at the others, they didn't initiate conversations. Kim and Brock had come to the same conclusion without consulting with each other. The other agents had to be leaving the plane here in the Montana capital because the President's newest hotel was here. The seventh place listed in the threat. While Kim and Brock were on their mission, these agents would be tackling their own agenda in the search for the bomb and some answers.

Brock turned to Kim once they were on the tarmac. "Let's go see about a rental car. According to Aaron's instructions, we still have an hour drive ahead of us."

Kim sighed as she raised her hands above her head and stretched. "I just want to get to the motel in Deer Valley. Flying always makes me tired."

Brock nodded. "I could use a soft bed myself. "
Staring at Kim, Brock frowned. "Are you hungry? I have a feeling that Deer Valley rolls up the carpets at sundown. I doubt if we'd find an all-night restaurant there. I think the town will be shut up tight by the time we drive in."

Kim shrugged. "I'm not hungry right now. Why don't we stop at a gas station and just grab some munchies and a drink for the drive."

Brock laughed. "You just described my favorite meal. C'mon let's go see about a vehicle first."

The two headed into the airport terminal. Although it sat in the capital city of Helena, the airport wasn't as large as the ones in Montana's bigger cities. Luckily the place still had all the amenities, including a car rental agency.

Stepping to the counter and asking for a vehicle, Brock was asked for his name.

When he gave it, the woman behind the
counter smiled broadly. "Your rental has
been taken care of Mr. Odom. I just need
your signature and then I can have our
customer service representative walk you
out to the vehicle."

A few moments later, a tall, thin man who to
both Brock and Kim looked about sixteen,
escorted them to the car Aaron had reserved.
Walking toward the dark colored SUV,
Brock couldn't get the sarcastic grin off his
face. Leave it to Aaron to make sure he was
driving something that fit into the FBI's
non-descript preference. Brock sighed, at
least it looked rugged enough to take on any
weather Montana might throw at him and
Kim as they completed their mission.

Accepting the keys from the young man and
thanking him, Brock frowned at Kim.
"Is it okay if I drive?'

Kim shrugged. "Be my guest. You're the
one from Montana."

Brock laughed. "What I remember could be
written down on a piece of paper and still
leave half the page blank."

The two took their places in the car. Brock drove away from the airport and to the first gas station he saw. Looking at the fuel gage, Brock smiled. "The car is full, let's go see if we can get some fuel for ourselves."

Going in the station, Brock and Kim grabbed chips and candy bars before both decided to grab a large coffee to keep them awake. Paying for the food and drinks, Brock got directions from the clerk before heading outside with Kim. She looked up at the sky and the first stars showing their face, before getting into the vehicle.
"I can see why they call Montana the big sky country. This is amazing."

Brock nodded, remembering the landscape along with beautiful sunrises and sunsets of Montana had been the things he missed after leaving the state.

The two got in the car and Kim shook her head. "I need this coffee now, but hope the caffeine wears off by the time we get to Deer Valley. I'm looking forward to a good night's sleep. I have a feeling it may be the last either of us get for a while."

Nodding, Brock grunted. "I'm afraid that goes with our job description. I've lost more sleep over the years than I care to admit."

Starting the car, Brock pulled away from the station and drove a half mile down the road where he turned on to a narrow, two lane highway and headed east.

Kim looked out her window frowning. "I hate flying through time zones." She lifted her wrist and looked at her watch. "Back home it's nine o'clock. I guess that makes it seven p.m. here."

Staring at the road ahead, Brock nodded. "It is strange. Better than flying from west to east though. You lose two hours that way, three if you're going coast to coast." Brock shrugged. "I think no matter what time it is, we should wait until morning to talk to Sheriff Danvers and try to find Cory Baxter."

Kim nodded. "I agree. I want to be fresh and wide awake for all that." Then she pointed ahead of them toward the mountains. "Look at that, the sun has almost finished going down. Hey, red sky at night, sailor's delight. Guess that's a good omen for tomorrow."

A grin crossed Brock's face. He could remember his grandfather using that saying. Brock was certain it didn't predict the future accurately half the time. The sunset was beautiful though and lent a warm feeling that emanated in the car. Brock nodded as the road turned from straight east to southeast.

A short time later, the sky was darker, but the landscape could still easily be seen. Kim once again pointed out the window, this time at Brock's side of the car. "Hey, is that the Missouri river?"

Brock nodded. "It is and just behind us was the Lewis and Clark National Forest. You're in the rugged west now, what do you think about it?"

The brown eyes opened wide. "I think it is amazing. How come you left Montana? This place is beautiful."

Brock nodded. "It is gorgeous, but the bigger cities had a lot more to offer a young man trying to make a living."

Nodding, Kim sighed. She had to admit no matter where you lived you would find good points and bad. She looked at her watch again. "We must be getting close."

Nodding, Brock pointed ahead and toward the east side of the highway where a few lights could be seen twinkling in the darker area. "I think that's Deer Valley. Just a few more minutes."

When Brock turned off the highway and entered the town of Deer Valley, finding the motel was easy. The town had a main street only three blocks long and the motel sign stood out with a flashing, vacancy sign.

Brock pulled in and parked, surprised, despite the vacancy sign, the parking lot had five or six cars filling it up.
Getting out of the car, the two walked in to get their rooms. Checking in only took a few minutes because Aaron had reserved the rooms for a whole week. Neither Brock nor Kim wanted their assignment to last that long, but were glad for Aaron's preparations in case they had a prolonged stay.
The rooms the two were given directions to were separate, but adjoining.

Carrying their bags in, Kim and Brock took a minute to examine the rooms. Kim was surprised to find the rooms large and clean with what she thought was local artwork adorning the walls. After she finished inspecting the room, Kim knocked on the adjoining door. Hearing Brock yell, 'come on in', Kim opened the door and stepped into a room identical to her own. She smiled at Brock. "I'm pleasantly surprised. These rooms are really nice."

Brock laughed. "All I care is that the bed feels just the way I like it."

Kim hadn't thought to try the bed, but took Brock's word for the comfort level. She yawned. "All I want to do is jump in the shower and get some sleep. Hope you don't mind my disappearing and not being good company."

Brock shook his head. "Don't worry about me. I'm going to check the news and then do the same. I'll see you in the morning. We can grab some breakfast before we head to the sheriff's office."

Kim nodded. "Sounds like a plan. Do you mind if I leave this door open a little? I hate waking up in strange places. Knowing your right here would make that easier."

Brock shrugged. "Okay by me, I'll try and not snore too loud."

Shaking her head, Kim laughed. "If you do, I'll come in and put a pillow over your face."

Turning, Kim went back to her room to prepare for bed.

Behind her, Brock turned on the TV, lowering the volume when he did. Flipping through the channels, Brock watched several of the twenty four hour news channels, listening for any word about the FBI already finding any of the bombs that had been talked about in the threat received.

After watching for an hour, Brock was satisfied nothing had happened yet, or at least nothing the press had found out about yet. Hoping it would stay that way, Brock turned off the television. Heading to the bathroom, Brock took his own shower.

Before climbing into bed, Brock pulled out his phone just long enough to send Aaron a text message stating the two had arrived.

Placing his phone on the bedside table, Brock adjusted his pillow and then let sleep overtake his tired body.

In her room, Kim took a few minutes to call her husband. When the two were separated, Kim only liked to call Blake and exchange the fact she had reached her destination. She liked to keep her work life separate from her home life. So, not sharing anything about her assignment, Kim checked in, traded an I love you, and then hung up, the sound of Blake's voice lingering in her mind and letting her fall into a sleep filled with good dreams.

Chapter 3

The next morning, Brock's internal alarm had him up early. He turned on the television again and watched for about an hour. Finding nothing important, Brock got dressed before looking through the partially opened door.

Kim was not only up and dressed, but she too was flipping through the channels. Turning to see Brock, Kim clicked off the TV and smiled. "Good morning. I hope you slept as well as I did."

Brock nodded. "Actually, surprisingly, I slept great. I can sleep anywhere, but being comfortable isn't always part of the equation. Are you ready for some breakfast?"

Nodding, Kim slipped on her shoulder holster and then added a light jacket over the top. "I'm ready now."

With his own holster already on beneath a vest, Brock grabbed a jacket from his room and the two stepped out into the cool morning air. Kim rubbed her arms. "I thought it would be warmer."

Brock laughed. "Just be glad there isn't snow. Montana weather is unpredictable."

After a quick, but hearty breakfast at a family style diner a block away from the motel, the two agents headed to the town's police station.

Entering the station they were greeted by an older woman seated behind a large, cluttered desk. "Good morning. What can I do for you?"

Brock pulled out his wallet and flashed his FBI ID and Badge. "I'm Agent Odom and this is Agent Mackey. Is Sheriff Danvers around?"

The woman nodded. "He said to watch for you. Take a seat and I'll get him."

The two sat down and watched as the woman got up from her desk and headed back into the station. Kim smiled and turned to Brock. "Nice to see person to person communication. Much better than calling or buzzing someone you want to talk to."

Although he hadn't thought about it, Brock nodded realizing Kim was right, you didn't see many people connecting in person anymore. The two looked up when a large man stepped into the room followed by the woman. The sheriff was in his late fifties with dark hair and eyes. The man was over six foot tall and carried about twenty extra pounds on his large frame.
While the woman sat back at her desk the man stepped over to the agents.
"I'm Sheriff Danvers. Director Jackson called and said to expect you. Come on into my office."

Standing, the two followed the sheriff down to a room. Letting the two inside, the sheriff closed the door behind them. "I thought we could use some privacy. Lucy, that's the lady out at the front desk. She's my receptionist and dispatch. Lucy is a great lady, but she likes gossip. Deer Valley is such a small town, word spreads fast."
The sheriff stuck out his hand and shook

first Kim's hand and then Brock's.
"I'd appreciate it if you two called me Walt.
From what your boss said, we might be
working together a day or two. Might as
well be on a first name basis. Go ahead and
take a seat."

Brock and Kim sat down in the wooden
chairs, while Walt moved around his desk
and took his own seat.
Brock was nodding at him. "Nice to meet
you Walt. I'm Brock and this is Kim. Aaron,
that is, Director Jackson, said you know
Cory Baxter."

Walt nodded. "I do, in fact, he's been a
guest in the jail a few times. Cory's not a
bad kid, just prone to trouble. Mostly he
likes to drink and then get in shouting
matches. Once in a while, those turn into all
out brawls. Other than that, nothing too
serious."
Walt sighed. "Aaron told me about the letter
and the threats. I know he has proof that
Cory mailed the letters, but he's right in
thinking Cory didn't write them. I can
almost guarantee that. I've known Cory a
long time. In fact since he was born. He's

had a hard time in life, but he just isn't the type to threaten anyone."

Kim frowned. "We're hoping Cory can help us find whoever is behind the threats. Someone had to have asked him to mail the letter. You will most likely have better luck talking to him than us. Especially if he finds out we're from the FBI."

Walt nodded. "I had the same thoughts myself. I thought we could all ride out to Cory's place and see what he has to say. No need to tell him you're agents unless he won't cooperate."

Kim and Brock nodded. Brock stood up. "Is now a good time?"

As soon as Kim stood beside Brock, Walt also stood. "It's a great time. I'd say Cory will still be sleeping. Hopefully we'll catch him off guard."

Leaving the station, the trio decided to take both the rented SUV and Walt's sheriff's car. Brock again drove with Kim in the passenger seat. Watching Walt pull out in the sheriff's car, Brock followed close behind. Brock and Kim were led a mile past the small sign stating they were leaving the Deer Valley city limits.

Looking at the sign as they drove past, Kim frowned. "That's funny, I guess I just assumed our suspect lived in Deer Valley."

Brock laughed. "I'm sure there's a large population outside Deer Valley that consider themselves citizens of the town. A lot of people like their privacy and move to the outskirts."

Kim shook her head. "It looked to me like you could live in the center of the town and still be on the edge of civilization."

Shaking his head, Brock grunted. "That's because you're a big city girl at heart."

Kim sighed. "I am that. I don't know how people get used to all the wide open space."

Brock smiled, but was watching the brake lights on the sheriffs car ahead of him flash on. "Looks like we must be getting close."

Brock slowed down while Kim sat up straighter, her attention also on the police car as it turned off the main road and onto a gravel driveway. Brock had to swerve several times around potholes before pulling in behind the sheriff's, now parked, vehicle.

The two waited for Walt to exit his car before they got out and joined him.

Walt pointed at the house in front of them. The single level home was partially obscured by overgrown trees and bushes. A small, open porch was semi-protected by a slanting, rusted metal roof. On either side of the front door, equal sized windows were dirty enough it was hard to tell if they had any type of covering on the inside.

The sheriff sighed. "Cory doesn't have much. His parents are both dead. His mom died in a car wreck when Cory was a teenager. His dad drank himself to death just a couple of years ago."
Walt didn't elaborate on the story he knew all too well. He'd known both Cory's mother and father. The three of them had gone to school together in Deer Valley. From Kindergarten all the way through their High School graduation. Walt and Cory's mom had dated in high school. She'd been Evie Graham back then. With his auburn

hair and green eyes, Cory resembled his mother. Evie had been the most beautiful girl Walt had ever seen. Her dark, reddish brown hair made her pale skin appear even lighter and almost the opposite of Walt's own bronze colored skin. Growing up, Walt had tried to ignore the name calling because of his Native American heritage. When he couldn't, Walt learned how to hold his own in the fights that ensued. Evie, not only didn't seem to mind the difference, but had seemed fascinated with Walt's background. Walt had fallen head over heels in love. He thought Evie had felt the same, but then Lance Baxter had stepped into the picture and everything changed. Lance was a braggart and although his family was just as poor as most others in Deer Valley, Lance always seemed to have money. He dressed nice, had a fast car and a line of bull that passed as sweet talk to Evie.

Despite reservations, Walt stepped aside and let Lance sweep Evie off her feet. Shortly after high school graduation, the two were married. The house the trio stood in front of in the cool Montana morning had been Evie's grandma's. A year after Evie and

Lance married, Evie inherited the house when her grandma died. The place wasn't fancy, but it was paid for. Lance didn't have a problem sharing the house with Evie and acting like it was his. He also didn't mind staying home while Evie worked.

The money Lance made came, not from a standard job, but from selling drugs. The town of Deer Valley didn't have many people who used drugs, but there were enough to give Lance money for the things he wanted. One of those things was spending most days and then nights sitting on a bar stool. When he finally returned home to Evie, more times than not, Lance was abusive. Still friends, Walt spent hours trying to get Evie to leave Lance when he found her with black eyes and even in the hospital twice with broken bones.

Evie denied that Lance was behind the bruises and broken bones. Making up excuses that both Evie and Walt knew were lies. When Evie got pregnant, the beatings stopped for a while, although Walt was sure she still suffered verbal abuse from her husband. Cory grew up alone most of the time. With Evie working a full time job, sometimes two, and Lance in the bar, Cory became a loner. He had been too ashamed to make friends and have them know of his home life. When Cory was fourteen, his mom and dad had been fighting. Cory had stayed in his room trying to avoid watching his mom being abused by his dad. Cory was afraid of Lance and at the time, not strong enough to stand up to the man. Lance had pulled Evie from the house and forced her into his car. When they drove away, Cory had no idea that would be the last time he saw his mom. With too much to drink, like usual, Lance had driven the car too fast around a curve. Hitting a tree, Lance had crawled from the wreck, but Evie never made it out of the crashed car.

During the next four years later, Cory found himself following in his dad's footsteps. Drinking to ease the pain and to shut out his father's berating him. When Lance had died from cirrhosis of the liver, Cory had been more relieved than sad. That feeling had him drinking even more.

Walt had stepped in, trying to help the young man that should have been his son.

He'd gotten Cory a job working at an auto repair shop to make ends meet. Walt hadn't been able to keep Cory away from the liquor or out of trouble though. Walt felt like he had failed not only Cory, but Evie, the only woman he had ever loved.

Standing outside the house that had once been Evie's and now belonged to her son, Walt's sense of failure tore at him, twisting his stomach into knots. He didn't think Cory had the ambition to plot out the bombing threats Agent Jackson had told him about, but Walt knew Cory was still in deep trouble.

Hoping the two agents weren't aware of his troubled thoughts, Walt stepped ahead and knocked on the door. Waiting a few moments with no answer, Walt knocked harder and then shouted. "Cory, damn it, I know you're in there. Answer this door or I swear I'll knock it down."

Behind Walt, Brock and Kim exchanged glances but didn't say anything. Deer Valley was Walt's jurisdiction and they needed his help. Interfering wouldn't get them anywhere and both knew that from other assignments they had been on.

Finally the door opened. A young man with dark auburn hair, that looked like it hadn't seen a comb in weeks, stood in the doorway. He was wearing only a pair of pajama bottoms. Wiping at his eyes, Cory tried to focus on not only Walt, but the two strangers standing behind him.
"Hey, there's no need to scream. You're giving me a headache. What's going on anyway Walt? It's a little early to have you banging on my door. I was asleep."

Walt shook his head. "It's not early and if you didn't have a hangover you'd realize that. I have some questions I need you to answer. I think you better let us inside."

The green eyes turned down in a frown, then filled with curiosity. "I don't know sheriff, I just don't let any strangers in my house. I haven't done anything wrong. What's this all about? Don't you need a search warrant to talk to me or something?"

Running a hand through his short dark hair, Walt's brown eyes filled with anger.

"If you know what's good for you, I think you better cut out the smart ass attitude and let us in."

Knowing not to anger Walt any further, Cory nodded and opened the door wider as he stepped back. "Sure Walt, I was just kidding. C'mon in. Who are your two friends?"

Walt shook his head. "Never mind who they are. We need to talk."
Turning back, Walt grinned at Brock and Kim, then winked as he motioned for them to follow him inside.

Stepping in the room after Walt, both Kim and Brock glanced around but ignored the mess in Cory's living room. The agents had both spent time in worst places.

Sitting down in a recliner, Cory motioned at a couch and the other chair in the room.
"Sit down. Sorry about the mess. Like I said, I just got up."

Walt took the chair, while Brock and Kim sat on the couch. A coffee table in front of them was covered with empty beer cans. Two bottles of whiskey also graced the surface. Both containers only had a sliver of amber liquid left of what had once been there.

Cory looked around at his visitors before letting his gaze land on the one face he recognized. "What did you mean we have to talk? You know me Walt, I've been staying out of trouble."

Walt shook his head. "I'm not so sure about that Cory. A short time ago you mailed a letter from the Deer Valley post office. That's why we're here this morning. We need to talk about that letter."

Cory frowned. "I mail a lot of letters. Do you think you could narrow it down a bit?" Cory's voice sounded angry, but when he reached out and grabbed a cigarette from the pack on the table, his shaking hands showed he was more nervous than mad.

Walt's dark eyes narrowed. "This is one you couldn't forget mailing. It was addressed to the FBI."

Cory started to shake his head, but stopped when Kim started speaking. "Cory, we have a picture of you mailing the letter. Surely you must know that even a post office in Deer Valley has video cameras."

Grabbing a lighter that sat next to the cigarette case, Cory held it, but didn't light his smoke. The green eyes widened. "That doesn't mean anything. The letter someone saw me mailing could have been going anywhere."

Leaning forward toward Cory, Walt looked like a predator closing in on its' much smaller prey. "Quit screwing with us Cory. We have proof the letter was addressed to the FBI."

Cory shrugged, the green eyes holding a bit of humor. "Okay, I mailed the letter. That's not against the law."

Walt stood quickly and moved over to stand so he was looking down on Cory. "It is when the letter includes bomb threats. You asked earlier who my friends were. Meet agents Brock Odom and Kim Mackey. They are from the FBI. Now, do you want to try this again and tell us about the letter?"

A sigh escaped Cory's mouth as he nodded slowly. "Okay, I mailed it. Listen, it was a joke. I was just screwing around okay. I'm not bombing any place. Hell, I wouldn't even know how."

The green eyes darted nervously from face to face. Cory wasn't sure what was happening. He'd mailed the letter, but he hadn't written it. He didn't even know the contents. The letter he'd been paid to mail had been sealed. He'd also already walked through the five thousand dollars he'd been paid for the task. At the time, the amount of money had stopped him from asking any questions. The fact that the sender had been willing to pay that much just for him to hand the letter to the clerk at the post office, also let Cory know he better keep his mouth shut. The man who had made the deal had just stopped him down in the garage where he worked and made the offer. Cory had never laid eyes on the guy before and hadn't seen him since. Cory wasn't the smartest guy around, but he knew he was in trouble. He had a feeling that although the man hadn't come back around, somehow he was watching. Just like the three people in the room were watching him right now.
Cory felt like throwing up.

He took a deep breath, held up the cigarette and lighter, then stood. "I'm just going to head outside for a smoke."

Reaching over, Walt grabbed Cory's elbow. "I think all of us could use some fresh air. We can talk outside."

Once outside, Cory hurried and lit his smoke and drew in a deep drag. He blew it out slowly, trying to think.

Still holding Cory's arm, Walt gripped it tight. "We want a name Cory. Who wrote that letter? I know it wasn't you."

Trying to pull away from Walt unsuccessfully, Cory shook his head. "I told you I wrote it, didn't I? What more do you want from me?"

Brock moved closer to the two men and stared at Cory. "You better listen to Walt. Admitting to writing that letter is a sure way to get yourself a federal prison sentence."

The green eyes widened, but Cory shook his head. He was still positive he had more to fear from the guy with the money that had started all this. He needed time to think and knew he wasn't going to get it.

"I don't have anything else to tell you. Maybe I should have a lawyer."

As soon as he uttered the words, Cory knew how accurate they were. Too bad he hadn't held on to some of the money, then he could have hired one.

Walt shook his head. "I'm not going to stand and listen to your lies Cory. Right now, you're under arrest. I'll let you head in and get dressed. After that, you can sit in the jail until you are ready to tell me the truth."

Walt looked at Brock and Kim.

"You two can follow us back to town. Just let me read Cory his rights. Let him change clothes and we can be on our way."

Kim and Brock listened as Walt recited the Miranda rights to Cory. He then followed Cory in the house and returned five minutes later. Walt once again grabbed Cory's elbow. Pulling him over, Walt placed him in the back of the patrol car. Once Cory was locked inside, Walt stepped back over to the agents. He kept his voice quiet so Cory couldn't overhear.

"A day or two in a cell and I think Cory will

tell us what you came to find out. I'm sorry
it's working out like this."

Brock laughed. "If the job was easy, it
wouldn't be fun. We'll meet you at the
station in a bit. I want to stop at the motel a
minute and call Aaron. Maybe some of the
other agents have had some luck."

Walt nodded, but was disappointed he
hadn't been able to get Cory to talk.
"I'll see you there."

Leaving Walt to handle Cory, Brock and
Kim backed out of the gravel driveway onto
the main road and headed for the motel.

With Cory locked in the backseat of his car,
a metal screen divider between them, Walt
was a first at a loss for words. He'd arrested
Cory before, but then the charges hadn't
been serious. With Cory facing something
Walt knew the young man couldn't deal
with, he also felt like he was letting Evie
down. After Evie's death, even when Lance
had still been alive, Walt felt a responsibility
to Evie to help watch over her only son.
Cory's father, Lance, had taught, by
example, his own bad habits. Each time

Cory had gotten into trouble, Walt had tried to find ways to set him straight and put him back on the right road. Today though, Walt worried that wasn't possible. Especially with Cory accepting responsibility for that damn letter. Walt turned slightly so he could keep an eye on the road while also focusing his attention on Cory.

"You better think about what you're doing here Cory. I don't know who wrote that letter or asked you to send it, but being part of a federal investigation is not the same as being thrown in jail for a barroom brawl. I want to help you Cory. More than you will ever know. I just can't do much without your cooperation. Protecting the person who gave you the letter isn't helping you. I'm sure you must realize that person is not going to come to Deer Valley and confess just to save your ass. You better do some long, hard thinking on this Cory. The FBI isn't going to sit on their hands and wait for you to come clean. If you continue to claim you not only mailed, but also wrote that letter filled with bomb threats, those two agents will lock you up. Federal prison is not a place you want to spend your time."

The car was silent. Walt waited a few moments to see if Cory would talk. By the time the sheriff pulled into the police station, Cory still hadn't spoken.

Walt parked the car and turned in his seat to stare into the green eyes. "You need to tell me the truth Cory. If you don't, there's no way I can help."

Cory stared back, but had nothing to say. He knew Walt was a good guy, but the man who had given him the letter was the one Cory was afraid of.

The slight shaking of Cory's bent head made Walt sigh. Opening his door, he got out of the car. Grabbing the handle of the back door, Walt pulled it open and took a hold of Cory's elbow. He hadn't bothered to handcuff the young man. He knew Cory wouldn't run. Right now, Walt almost wished the young man would try to escape. Walt knew he would let him go if he did. He was scared for Cory's future and only hoped Cory knew how serious the situation was.

Walt sighed. "Come on Cory. Time to book you into a cell. I hope with all my heart you can sort this out and do the right thing."

Cory remained silent, but his mind was reeling as Walt pulled him into the station.

Chapter 4

Heading to the motel, Brock and Kim decided to use Brock's room to make the call to Aaron. The agents each took a seat in the straight back chairs.

Brock pulled out his phone and called Aaron Jackson's private number. The call was answered right after the first ring. The familiar voice could be heard by both Brock and Kim over the speaker phone Brock had turned on. "Brock, I'm glad you called. How's the assignment going?"

Neither Brock nor Kim were surprised by Aaron's 'right to business' attitude. Brock looked at Kim, a half grin on his face. "Hi Aaron, Kim's here with me and we're both okay. Thanks for asking."

The two could here Aaron's hearty chuckle. "Sorry about that. I'm glad to hear you're good. What about Cory Baxter? Any luck?"

Brock shrugged. "Not as much as we'd like. The sheriff helped us out. It seems he knows Cory fairly well. The kid isn't talking though."

Kim nodded and interrupted Brock. "It took a bit of talking just to get Cory to admit he sent the letter. Sadly, he is sticking to the story he wrote it."

Brock sighed. "Which makes no sense. We even let him know he was looking at Federal prison time."

Back in D.C., Aaron was tapping his pencil on his desk in agitation. "The only reason I can think of for that is Cory Baxter is more afraid of the person that had him mail the letter than he is of prison time."

Kim drew in a breath. "Oh hell, that doesn't sound good. We could be dealing with a lot worse than a person who is mentally unstable. The letter writer could be someone real powerful."

Brock nodded. "Or belong to a group that is. There seem to be a lot of new crazy unconventional groups now a days."

Aaron sighed. "That's true, but most of those people are backers of the President. Remember the bomber is trying to repair the damage the President has done."

Kim was nodding. "And the President's new hotel is the last place on the list to be bombed. Why would groups that like the man want to kill him?"

Shaking his head, Aaron grunted. "That's what the two of you need to find out. I should tell you the agents in California will be heading into the Universal Access studio tonight. We're hoping to avoid publicity."

Kim groaned. "That's going to be almost impossible. The place is a gossip news agency."

Brock was frowning. "The bomb isn't supposed to be set off until tomorrow. What if the mechanism isn't set up in the building yet?"

Aaron sighed. "Then the agents will be sleeping in the building. We can't take any chances. I think the bomb is probably already there and with a remote detonator. Either way, we'll be ready."

Brock nodded and blew out his breath. "Good luck to them then. Kim and I are heading back to the station. The sheriff will have Cory booked in by now. Hopefully being in the jail cell will help him decide he's in more trouble from the law than he is from whoever told him to mail that letter."

Back in his office, Aaron stood from his desk. "Lean on this kid if you have to. Try a good cop, bad cop, routine. Maybe Kim can connect with Cory's sensitive side. I'll try to call and update you, but you should keep the news on too. I'm sure you remember Universal Access likes to drop their own kinds of bombs. That's the first target on the bomber's list. You two watch your backs and good luck."

Looking over at Brock, Kim sighed and nodded. "Good luck to all of us."

Turning off the phone, Brock stood. Looking over at Kim, he shrugged. "You heard the boss. Let's get back to the jail."

Standing herself, Kim shook her head before running her hands through her short blonde hair. "I know Aaron said to try the good cop, bad cop routine. I hate to tell you this, but despite appearances, I'm really not the best at being nice."

Staring into the brown eyes that right now looked honest and innocent, Brock laughed. "Kim, the way you look, no one would ever think of you as a bad cop."
Despite saying that, Brock knew Kim was trained to fight, both with and without a gun and she was dangerous. He envied her the edge her looks gave her.

With a shrug, Kim gave Brock back an uneven grin. "I hope you're right and that Cory Baxter sees me the same way. Maybe we can get some information out of him after all."

Brock frowned. "To tell you the truth, I think Walt might have better luck with that than either of us. He said he knew Cory and that he'd even held Cory in his jail several times. I get the feeling there's more to their relationship than that. Watching those two was like watching a protective relative keeping an eye over a family member."

Kim sighed. "I just want answers no matter how we come by them."

Brock nodded. "Let's go then. I'll even buy you a cup of coffee on the way."

Rolling her eyes, Kim laughed. "Nice to be partnered up with such a big spender. I'll take what I can get."

Leaving the motel, the agents headed to the gas station to grab their coffee before heading to the police station.

Lucy once again greeted the two as they stepped in. "Walt is expecting you. He said for you to head back to his office. Do you remember the way?"

Brock and Kim nodded and thanked the woman before walking past her desk to Walt's closed door. Brock's knock was answered quickly by Walt's hollered, "Come on in."

When Brock pushed open the door, Walt stood. He pointed at the cups the two were holding. "If you need a refill, we always have a pot on. If not, we might as well get this over with and go see Cory."

Shaking their heads at the offer of a refill, Brock and Kim followed Walt to the back of the station.

Leading the way, Walt twisted his head backwards as he spoke to the agents while they walked. "Cory was silent, not only on the drive, but he didn't say a word while I booked him in either. I hope sitting in that cell will make him wake up to the seriousness of the situation."

Kim was nodding. "I hope you're right. Director Jackson has agents out watching over the locations of the bomb threats, but it sure would help if we had the name of whoever gave Cory that letter."

Brock frowned. "If Cory is giving you the silent treatment we might not be able to get him to talk right now. If that happens, we'll take off for the evening. Hopefully we'll find in the morning a long night of sitting and worrying will loosen his tongue."

Nodding, Walt stopped at a desk with an officer in uniform sitting behind it. The sheriff nodded at the man. "Deputy Carlyle, meet agent Odom and agent Mackey. The

FBI has asked them to help us out. They're going to be a round a day or two. I want you to treat them like one of our own."

The deputy stood and shook both agents hands. He tried to not let his surprise show at seeing FBI agents in Deer Valley. Walt had booked Cory Baxter in himself and hadn't shared any detail of the arrest. At the moment, Cory was the only prisoner in the six cell jail. Deputy Carlyle cleared his throat. "It's an honor to meet both of you. If you need anything, just give me a holler."

Walt reached on the wall next to the desk and grabbed a large key ring with several keys on it. "Right now, this is all we need."

The deputy nodded and watched the three walk away toward the cells. The surprise and admiration at having the agents in the jail left him at a loss for more words. He sat back down overwhelmed.

Neither Brock nor Kim noticed the deputy's predicament, they were too busy following Walt as he headed to Cory's cell.

Approaching the six by eight foot room, the three could see Cory sitting on the bed through the metal bars that made up the front of the cell. He was sitting on the cot with his head resting in his hands. If he heard the sound of his visitors, Cory didn't give any reaction. Unlocking the door, Walt pulled it open to let Kim and Brock enter first. Stepping in behind the agents, Walt closed and locked the door.

Brock noticed someone, probably Walt, had set up three chairs in the room. Brock motioned for Kim to take her choice first. When she did, Brock sat beside her with Walt taking the remaining seat.

Since she was supposed to play the good guy part of the scenario, Kim cleared her throat and spoke first. "Cory, I want you to know agent Odom and I are here to help you. I think it would be easier if we stayed on a first name basis. I'm Kim and my partner is Brock. Before we start, I'd like to tell you I'm sorry to hear about your parents. It's hard when you don't have family around."

The head of reddish brown hair lifted and green eyes glared at Kim. "Save your pity lady. I don't want you feeling sorry for me.

If you and your pal there are going to charge me with something, just go ahead and do it. I already told you, I mailed that letter and wrote it too. You may not believe I'm smart enough, but I am. It was just a joke okay. I didn't even think the FBI would get the letter."

Across from Cory, now it was Kim who was glaring. If looks could kill, Cory would no longer be alive. She lifted a hand and pointed a finger at Cory. "Listen you little punk. I came in here to try and help you. I'd advise you to change that attitude of yours and get some respect. Brock and I can help you, but you'll find we can also be your worst enemy."

Beside Kim, Brock was frowning. "Don't waste your breathe Kim."
He stared at Cory. "Here's what I want from you. I don't need to hear it word for word, but I want you to tell me just what you wrote in that letter. The only way you can prove to us you're the author is to do that."

The green eyes wandered, looking everywhere but at the sheriff and the two agents as Cory tried to settle his nerves and think back to what the sheriff and the agents had told him about the letter earlier. "I was mad at the FBI, I sent the letter threatening to bomb their headquarters. Listen, I didn't mean it. I know I was wrong, but honest, I wasn't going to do anything. Hell, I don't know nothing about bombs."

The two agents and the sheriff stared at Cory in disbelief. The young man had no idea what was in the letter nor how much trouble he was in.

Brock let out a grunt of disbelief. "Not even close Cory. Do you want to try again or are you ready to come clean and tell us who gave you that letter to mail?"

Crossing his arms over his chest, Cory shook his head. "I don't have anything else to say to any of you."

Brock shrugged. "Fine with me. To tell you the truth, it's past my dinner time and I get ornery when I'm hungry."
Brock turned to Kim. "What about you, could you use some food?"

Kim nodded. "Yeah, now that you mention it. Grabbing dinner sounds a whole lot better than sitting here and listening to the garbage Cory is spouting."

Brock's face was serious, but Kim could see the sparkle in his eyes as he nodded and stood. "Let's get out of here then."
He looked over at the sheriff. "Walt, you want to let us out of here? Kim and I will be back in the morning and see if Cory has changed his mind. If he's gonna stick to his story, then we can transfer him into a Federal Prison. Of course, if any of those seven bombs go off, you know, the ones Cory seems to have forgotten about, well then, I guess we'll be locking Cory up and throwing away the key."

Without giving Cory a chance to answer, the sheriff nodded and stood. He realized what Brock was doing and hoped by morning Cory would do some hard thinking about Brock's words.

The three stepped out of the cell. Brock and Kim waited while Walt locked the cell door and then followed him past the deputy toward the front of the police station.

Walt led the agents to his office. Once all were settled in their chairs, Walt shook his head. "I'm really sorry about the way that went. Cory has been in trouble through the years, but I have never seen him act like that. Despite my arresting him, Cory always held respect for the office I hold."
Walt shook his head. "I just can't explain his attitude."

With a sigh, Brock shook his head. "He's scared Walt. I think he's deathly afraid of whoever asked him to mail that letter. Think about it. Someone singled Cory out, more than likely paid him, probably more money than a young man like Cory ever saw before. Cory must feel he's in more danger from that person than he is from the law or justice. We've told him he could be sent to federal prison. Let's give him the chance to think that over tonight. Kim and I will be back in the morning and see if his attitude has changed. Don't think his attitude is a reflection on you. Hell, both Kim and I have seen a lot worse. I think the best thing is for us to head back to the motel. If you want to try and talk to Cory that's fine, but I think some more sitting alone in that cell is the best medicine right now."

Not sure what was the best course of action, Walt let out a sigh as he reluctantly nodded. "Maybe you're right. I think I will have a little talk with him, but then Cory's future is up to him. He's not a bad person, I think he will come to the right conclusion."

Kim shrugged. "I hope your right. Time is running out. That first bomb is set to go off tomorrow. I think the agents in Southern California will stop the explosion, but six more will be coming. The bomber said one a day. We need to find the man behind that letter."

Walt nodded as Brock and Kim stood. Brock reached over the desk and held out his hand. Walt stood and took the offered hand and shook it. Green eyes stared into brown. "No matter what happens, I want to thank you for your help Sheriff. Believe me, not every police jurisdiction is good to the FBI."

Walt smiled. "Then they're fools. I appreciate both of you being here and I think we'll get to the bottom of this."

Kim and Brock left Walt sitting in his office.
The two stopped and grabbed a pizza before
heading back to the motel.

The two sat in Kim's room to eat their
dinner. The television was on, turned to the
twenty four hour news channel. Thankfully
nothing about the letter or the bombings had
leaked out yet.

After his third piece of pizza, Brock leaned
back in the chair and rubbed his stomach.
"I think I ate too much."

Kim laughed. "I only had one and I'm
stuffed. I don't know where you put it."
The brown eyes turned serious. "I suppose
they should be all set up at the Universal
Access Studios. How do you think they'll
do?"

Brock shrugged. "I don't think they'll have a
problem finding the bomb. I worry more
about any backlash if anything goes wrong.
The way things are now, a lot of the public
is losing faith in the FBI and the other
intelligence agencies."

The brown eyes narrowed in anger.
"You can give the President the credit for

that. If he wouldn't have talked down the special council investigation, things would be different."

Brock nodded, glad no one was around to hear either of them talking about the President. "I still can't believe the congress dropped their investigation on that. Everyone knows he lied. So much time and effort putting the proof together of his collusion and money laundering to have the reports just ignored and thrown away. To think it will be the President who is in danger from the last bombing and we are the ones saving him is ridiculous."

Kim nodded. "Hopefully that will give the pubic a better picture of what we do and show them we aren't politically biased." Kim rolled her eyes. "Hell, I've worked with people for years and still don't know how they vote or even care."

Sitting up in his chair and stretching, Brock nodded. "I know exactly what you mean. All we can do is perform our job the best way we know how. Hopefully time will change how people feel."

Kim smiled. "Yeah and maybe one of these days the truth will come out."

Yawning, Brock nodded. "Right now, I need to get some sleep. Must have been all that food I ate. All of a sudden I feel like I could sleep for a week."

Kim started laughing. "You get what you asked for. Go on and get some rest. I'm going to sit up for a bit and watch the news. I'll see you in the morning."

Joining in the laughter, Brock felt the worries of the day lift. "See you tomorrow. Sleep well Kim."

Chapter 5

The sound entered into Brock's dream and blended in. He was walking on the beach alone. The serenity of the place in itself, should have calmed him. Instead, Brock couldn't shake the feeling of sensory overload. He held a handful of sand in his clenched fist. Opening his hand, Brock let the particles slide through his fingers. Instead of fine sand, it was like sandpaper was scraping the skin. Beneath his feet, instead of warming his soles, the sand left a burning sensation. Looking ahead, the bright sun had Brock closing his eyes against the blinding glare. Drawing in a breath through his nose, the smell of the salt water should have been faint if noticeable at all. Brock frowned, wondering what was causing his senses to be on such a heightened alert. The loud noise that startled him just seemed to be a part of the other strange feelings he was suffering with. He glanced around in search of the source, hoping to be able to silence the intrusion. Not seeing anything, Brock turned quickly, feeling the sensation of something behind him. The motion jolted him from his dream.

Shaking away the dream, Brock realized the noise had followed him out. Realizing the noise wasn't part of the dream, but his cell phone, Brock frowned. Flinging out a hand, Brock reached blindly on the nightstand. Feeling his phone, Brock snatched it up and answered.

"Whoever this is, it better be important."

On the other end of the line, Aaron didn't have the time or temperament for sympathy. "Damn straight it's important. Get out of bed and turn on your TV. That will save me some explaining."

Sitting up on the side of the bed, Brock turned on the lamp before reaching for the television's remote control. Hitting the button, Brock squinted at the bright screen. Brock quickly read the scrolling headlines beneath the breaking news banner at the bottom of the screen. Brock's eyes went from the printed words, to focus on the

reporter's face giving the story.
He could feel his heart speed up as the words sunk in and burned into his mind,

"President slams the FBI's latest bungled investigation."

The reporter was standing outside and just beneath the sign reading 'Universal Access Studios'.

Moving to the foot of the bed, Brock sat, leaning toward the TV riveted. Out of the corner of his eye, Brock saw movement by the door connecting his room to Kim's. Glancing in her direction, Brock took the time to motion for Kim to enter and then pointed toward the TV.
Moving in the room and sitting on the bed next to Brock, Kim didn't speak. She could see Brock held his phone in a clenched fist, but he wasn't speaking into it at the moment.

Brock had already turned back to the screen, green eyes wide, the drowsiness from earlier, erased by the phone call and the news events happening on the television.

As the reporter continued speaking, Kim also stared at the image in front of her.

"From our own reports, we can tell you the FBI agents are still in the building. One bomb has been removed from the Universal Access Studios and taken away. We're told at this time the area has been secured and is safe. This channel has been able to obtain exclusive reporting that there is more to this story than meets the eye. The President has sent out an early morning tweet and I quote. "Another Fake FBI investigation. Their search for phony tapes has come up with nothing. Fake News." Our station has uncovered that although the FBI did indeed remove a bomb, their main goal was to search the Universal Studio's vault of archived tapes. More on that story as we get it. This is Jack Testman reporting from the Universal Access Studio in Southern California. Back to you Natalie."

Brock turned off the TV and turned his attention to the phone. "What the hell is going on Aaron? How in the hell does the President already know about all this?"

Inside the Universal Access Studio building, Aaron was staring at the door to the room the reporter had just been reporting on. A huge, brand new, padlock held the door closed. The FBI agents had only started searching the room when the studio's owner had rushed in brandishing a court order in one hand and motioning to a police officer with the other. The FBI operation had been shut down.

Aaron was shaking his head. "Who in the hell knows. We removed the bomb, which wasn't active although it did have a remote control triggering device. We didn't share that news and The Universal Studio people were falling over backwards thanking us for stopping the bombing. Under the pretense of searching for more bombs, we entered the studio's archive room. That's when all hell broke loose. I don't know how the owner was able to get a Federal Judge to issue a cease and desist order so quickly, but he did."

Glancing over at the curious Kim, Brock could only shake his head at the questioning look that darkened her brown eyes.

Speaking into the phone, Brock's green eyes, echoed that look. "You just said we. Aaron what are you doing in Southern California?"

Aaron half grinned. "What do you think, I'm going to sit in my office and let the field agents have all the fun? I'm definitely staying hands on in this investigation. Especially now with the President playing with that damn twitter account of his."

Brock didn't try to stop his own grin, despite seeing the deep frown lines on Kim's face as she studied the action.

Brock nodded. "Glad to hear you say that and know that I'm not the only one that feels that way."
Brock hadn't heard Aaron disparage the President before. In fact, it had only been a couple of days ago when Aaron had warned Brock not to get caught saying anything against the man who ran the country. Aaron's words let Brock know just how upset the director truly was. "So, what's next?"

Aaron half grunted. "I'm headed back to Washington. The second bomb is supposed to be hidden in the office of Housing and Urban development. You and Kim are going to get some answers from Cory Baxter."

Brock nodded. "We'll head over to the jail this morning. What about the third threat? Are you headed to the President's property in Florida?"

A deep sigh could be heard before Aaron answered. "I don't think I can make it to that one. The fourth location for the bombs is the Secretary of State's office here in Washington. I'll be needed there. The agents can handle the property in Florida. Hopefully, all the bombs will be fakes, but we can't rely on that. Listen, I need to get going. Just make sure to keep me in the loop with Cory Baxter and keep an eye on the news."

Brock sighed. "The same advice to you Aaron. Stay safe."

Brock hung up the phone and turned to Kim explaining what had happened, knowing Kim had only been privy to his side of the

conversation and the news report on TV.
When he finished, Brock exhale noisily.
"We need to get to the jail. Whatever it takes
we need to get Cory talking."

Kim stood. "Just give me a minute to get
dressed. We can grab some coffee on the
way. My treat this time."

Less than an hour later, Kim and Brock
walked into the police station. Greeted once
again by Lucy, the two were told to head
into the sheriff's office.

Walking down the hall the two found the
door to the sheriff's office standing open.
Walt stood as soon as Brock and Kim
approached. His first words let both of them
know he had been expecting them.
"I saw the news."
Walt shook his head. "It's a terrible and
dangerous thing for the President to demean
the intelligence and law enforcement
agencies. I made sure that Cory saw the
breaking news on the television. I think he
might be a little more willing to talk with the
two of you this morning. C'mon I'll take
you back."

The trio walked together to the desk sitting in front of the cells where they had been the night before. A different deputy manned the desk, but this time Walt didn't bother with introductions. Grabbing the keys from the wall, Walt stepped quickly away from the desk and toward Cory's cell with the agents as close behind as possible. The agents were having a hard time keeping up with Walt's longer strides. As Walt opened the cell door, the two behind him could see Cory was in almost the exact position he had been when they had last seen him.

Letting Kim and Brock enter first, Walt locked the door before also stepping in. The three folding chairs used the night before were still in place.
Brock took the one directly facing Cory and waited for Kim and Walt to sit on either side of him before he leaned forward toward Cory and began speaking.
"Walt tells us you were allowed to watch the news earlier. I hope that helped you realized how dire your situation is. The bomb threats are no game and more are coming."

The bowed head lifted and green eyes filled
with fear stared at Brock. The eyes closed as
the head bobbed up and down slightly.
When Cory spoke his words were barely
above a whisper. "I'm scared. You were
right. I didn't write that letter. I admit I
mailed it. I got paid five thousand dollars."
Cory grunted. "Five thousand to mail a
damn letter. Can you imagine? I jumped at
the chance. Someone with money like that to
throw around isn't going to like my talking.
Damn it, he'll kill me. I'd rather rot away in
the federal pen. At least I'd be breathing."

Brock sighed and tried to speak in a calm,
reassuring voice. Only his clenched fists
belayed how worried he was. "We'll protect
you Cory. We can have an agent stay with
you twenty four seven. We have safe houses
set up all over the country. We can move
you into one. We have to stop this bomber.
The agents were lucky this morning to get to
that bomb in time, but there are more
coming." Brock didn't share the knowledge
he had that the first bomb was phony.
"If you would have read that letter, you'd
know there are seven bombs scheduled to go
off. The bomber threatened a bomb a day to

make his point. A lot of innocent people could die. You can prevent that. We need that name Cory."

The eyes staring at Brock were red from tiredness and worry. Cory shook his head. "What if you can't protect me? I don't want to die."

Next to Brock, Walt reached out a big hand and placed it on Cory's leg. "If your mom was here, I know she'd be more worried about the other innocent lives that are in danger. If you protect them, the agents can protect you. I know you inherited your mother's compassion Cory. You know the right thing to do. Trust Brock and Kim. They didn't take you away from here already because they hoped you would do what was right. What's this guy's name Cory?"

Looking at Walt, Cory was reminded of all the times the sheriff had helped him since first his mom, then his dad, had passed away. Cory had never asked Walt why, but had wondered about the reasoning behind Walt's compassion several times. Now it was too late to delve into the motives. Cory also knew he owed Walt big time for all he did. Staring at Walt, Cory sighed, knowing no matter what he did. Life would never be the same. Finally, he nodded.

"The guy brought his car into the shop. We had to order parts, so he stayed in town overnight. It was after his car was finished and he was getting ready to leave that he asked me to mail that letter. He told me it would be worth my while and handed me the cash. I knew that something illegal had to be involved, but I didn't care."

Cory shook his head. "You don't know what holding five thousand in cash was like. It didn't take much convincing for me to agree to the deal."

Kim grinned. "Don't feel bad Cory. That guy knew for that kind of money just about anyone would have done the same thing." Kim frowned. "Did this guy tell you his name?"

Cory shook his head. "No, but his name was on the receipt. I probably wouldn't have remembered it, but it was familiar to me. You see, I love baseball, especially the Boston Red Sox. The guy's name was

Daniel Ortiz, you know, like he was related to the Red Sox team's old designated hitter. I can describe him to you if you want."

Reaching in his pocket and pulling out a small notebook and a pen, Brock nodded. "We can do that, go ahead and tell me what you remember. Hopefully we can get an idea and something we can run through the system."

Feeling Walt's hand gripping his leg tighter in a gesture of warmth, Cory turned to see the sheriff smiling at him. "You're doing the right thing Cory."

Giving Walt a half grin, Cory turned back Brock. "I don't think the guy is from America. He had a funny accent and his speech was a bit choppy. The guy was an inch or two shorter than me, maybe five eight. He outweighed me by twenty or thirty pounds though. He was heavy, but not fat, more like what you would call stocky." Cory frowned, thinking about the man who had handed him five thousand dollars to mail a letter. "Dark hair and eyes. In fact I think his eyes were even darker than his hair. Not much difference between that color

and his black pupils."
Silent a few seconds, Cory's brown eyes lit up. "The guy had a tattoo. When he handed me the envelope, I saw it. On his left hand, he had a snake."

Shaking his head, Brock smiled. "That's a damn good picture you're painting of the guy. Thanks a lot Cory."
Slipping his notebook and pen in his pocket, Brock stood. "I'm going to give Aaron a call. Maybe we'll get lucky and find out this guy was dumb enough to use his real name. I'll give Aaron the privilege of running the guy through NCIC. Even with just a name and the description Cory gave us, the national crime information center might find something. I wish we had more to go on."

Standing quickly, Cory stared at Brock, his green eyes wide. "I do have more, at least I think I do. The car the man was driving who asked me to mail that letter had Florida plates. I don't know how much you know about cars, but that guy had a lot of money tied up in that vehicle. It was a fifty six BMW, five oh three. And it was in mint condition. We're talking a two to three hundred thousand dollar car."

Shaking his head, Brock whistled loudly. "I think that information will be a big help. Thanks a lot Cory. I sure am glad you're into cars."

Smiling, Cory sat back down while Brock turned and walked out of the cell, leaving the door unlocked and partially open.

Cory, Walt and Kim remained in the cell after Brock left. Kim couldn't imagine what was going through Cory's mind. By the look on his face, the young man was scared to death. She gave him what she hoped was a reassuring smile. "Things are going to work out Cory. You should be proud of the choices you're making. You already saw this morning the bomber wasn't just making idle threats. Your cooperation could potentially save hundreds of lives."

Drumming his fingers on jittering legs, Cory let out a sigh. He nodded at Kim, but was finding coming up with words hard. It took a minute before he cleared his throat and began speaking. "I owe you an apology. I'm

sorry I talked to you the way I did yesterday.
That was wrong. I'm not like that. I know
it's a dumb excuse, but I really was scared."
Cory grunted. "Hell, I'm still afraid."

Lifting a shoulder, Kim half shrugged.
"Don't worry about it. I've had hundreds of
prisoners who gave me a much harder time.
I try not to take anything personal.
Although, if it makes you feel better, your
apology is accepted and you're forgiven."

Cory smiled. "Thanks, that does make me
feel better."

The three looked up as Brock stepped in the
doorway. "Aaron is running the name. He's
been having a lot of problems back in
Washington though."

Kim frowned. "Oh hell, A bomb didn't
explode did it?"

Brock shook his head. "No, and they didn't
expect one until tomorrow. Brock decided
with the first incident going so wrong, he
wanted to head into all the places on the list
early and look for the bombs before more
problems came up. Agents were able to get
into four of the six remaining places, but are

having problems at the two properties owned by the President. In Florida and the one here in Montana the people managing the property are saying Aaron needs the president's permission and a warrant."

Kim shook her head. "That doesn't make any since. Aaron had to have told them they were under a bomb threat."

Nodding, Brock blew out a disgusted breath. "Apparently they weren't convinced. I do have some good news. Aaron has a safe house in Helena where we can take Cory. He wants both of us up there also. We're going to connect with the agents trying to get in the hotel and see if we can help convince the manager the kind of danger the place and the people in and around it are in."

A frown wrinkled Walt's brow. He had been hoping that Cory could stay in Deer Valley. Walt wanted to be the one to protect Evie Graham's son. He felt he owed the woman at least that much. He also knew realistically Cory was better off in the FBI's hands. Walt stood. "If Cory is being moved to Helena, he might want to travel in something besides that orange jumpsuit he's wearing."

A smile covered Cory's face as he nodded. "That sounds like a good idea. I almost forgot I was wearing the jail issued clothes."

Standing, Cory followed Walt from the cell. As soon as the two were gone, Kim turned to stare at Brock. "Do you think it was a good idea talking about what Aaron and the other agents are doing in front of Cory?"

Brock shrugged. "Who's he going to talk to? For now, Cory is with us and once we get to Helena, he'll be under another agents' supervision. Besides, I think the more he realizes the danger he's in, the better off he'll be."

The sound of Brock's phone echoed in the cell chamber. Brock frowned.
"That's a text."
Pulling out his phone, Brock looked at his message and grinned. "Looks like the guy with the famous BMW that so impressed Cory used his legal name after all."
Brock turned to stare at Kim. "According to Aaron, Daniel Ortiz is an immigrant from

Haiti. He's in America on a work visa. He also has had his hands in the wrong cookie jar more than once. The guy's been arrested twice for burglary. You're not going to believe who he works for and where?"

Kim frowned, but didn't speak as she waited for Brock to share the information he had received.

Shaking his head, Brock grunted. "Mr. Ortiz is currently employed by our President, or rather his sons. At least that's what the President tells people. Personally, I think he is still the owner. Anyway, Many Lakes resort is in Florida. Aaron has instructed the agents to look for him there. That is if they can get inside the resort."

The brown eyes staring at Brock narrowed. "He works for the President? I'm beginning to think we're being led on a wild goose hunt."

Slipping his phone back in his pocket, Brock sighed. "Maybe, but those bombs are too damn real. All we can do right now is get Cory some place safe and link up with the agents in Helena. Hopefully by the time we do that, Aaron will have more information for us to work with."

Nodding, Kim stood. "Let's go see if Cory is ready and let Walt know the newest facts."

Chapter 6

Ten minutes later, Brock and Kim had joined Walt and Cory in the station's break room. Cory was dressed in his street clothes and listening while Brock explained everything he and Kim had learned to Walt.

When they finished, Walt shook his head, the dark eyes glanced from one agent to the other filled with concern. "With all the new developments, maybe Cory should stay here in the jail. Not as a prisoner, but for his own safety."

Brock shook his head. "I know you want him where you can keep an eye on him, but the FBI is trained to protect people. I'm sorry Walt, but I think taking Cory to Helena is the best way to safeguard him."

With a sigh, Walt nodded. "I know you're right. I just wish there was a way to keep him here."

Looking at Walt, Cory smiled. "I have faith in your abilities Walt and I appreciate the offer, but I think Brock is right. Besides, I still broke the law. Only the FBI will be able to fix that. Hopefully, as a witness, I'll be able to get out of this mess without any more damage done."
Cory frowned. "What about grabbing some things from my house? Can I do that?"

Kim shook her head. "That's not advisable right, now. Later, after you're settled and safe you can contact Walt and have him get what you need."

Reluctantly, Cory nodded, knowing Kim was right.

Turning to look at Brock, Walt frowned. "Where are you parked at?"

Lifting a hand, Brock motioned toward the far side of the room they were all standing in. "I parked in the lot on the side of the building."

Walt nodded. "Let's take the back door. We can hopefully slip out of here unnoticed. I don't feel like answering any questions right now."

The others nodded their understanding of what Walt was saying and followed Walt to the station's back door.

Stepping to the door, Walt and Cory moved out first, followed by Brock and Kim.

Pointing to the right, Brock turned to look at the others. "I'm in the middle of the lot over there."

The four started walking, this time with Brock and Kim leading the way. Walt and Cory stayed close behind.

The sound of a gunshot, had Brock and Kim reaching under their light jackets for the pistols hidden in their shoulder holsters. Instead of grabbing the pistol on his side, Walt's hands were suddenly full as he reached out, trying to prevent Cory from dropping to the ground.

The sound of Walt screaming Cory's name blended with the noise of a second shot. Walt felt the young man's body jerk with the second impact. Something he had neither seen nor felt when Cory had been hit the first time. Cradling Cory's body, Walt dropped to the ground.

Brock began running toward the area where the shot had come from. Kim, torn between wanting to help Cory and needing to find the shooter, yelled at Walt. "Stay with Cory." Then she also took off running, following the same path Brock had taken.

On the ground, Kim's words had barely registered to Walt. Staring down at Cory, Walt could see the blood stain spreading across the boy's chest. Although Cory was twenty three, he would always be a boy to Walt. Staring at Cory's closed eyes and listening to his labored breathing, Walt knew in his heart that Cory would remain that age forever. Removing one hand from where it rested against Cory's back, Walt readjusted his legs so Cory laid on his lap. Ignoring the blood covering his hand, Walt carefully brushed the auburn hair off Cory's forehead. "Hang on Cory. You're going to be okay."

The green eyes opened just enough that Walt could make out the color through Cory's lashes. The sigh that sounded turned into a cough as Cory struggled to speak. "I'm dying."

A bout of coughing had Walt clenching Cory's shoulders. "Don't talk, just rest."

The coughing stopped as Cory spoke the last words he ever would on this earth. "I'll tell mom you said hi."

The eyes closed and Walt felt Cory's body go limp. Staring at the body that covered his lap, Walt felt tears sting his eyes. Lost in grief, he didn't hear his deputy nor his dispatcher, Lucy, running toward him.
Even though Lucy was yelling, Walt barely heard the words.
"The ambulance is on the way. What happened out here?"
Lucy stepped closer and her face crumbled seeing Cory and knowing there was no life left in his body. "Oh no, oh my God, no."

Walt finally looked up. "Get back inside. The shooter is still out here. Brock and Kim went after him."

The deputy grabbed Lucy's arm and pulled her back toward the building just as the sound of an ambulance siren sliced through the air.

Once again, Walt returned his attention to Cory. "I'm so sorry. I should have kept you safe. Please forgive me."
Walt's head dropped as he mumbled one more sentence. "I hope you can forgive me too Evie."

The sound of steps had Walt looking up again. Thinking Lucy had returned, Walt was ready to shout at her to get to safety. His eyes widened seeing Brock and Kim each clutching an elbow of the man who walked between them. Walt could see the man's shirt from the right shoulder on down the sleeve was soaked in blood.
Kim was carrying an extra gun and a cell phone that Brock had stripped from the man after he had shot him.
Hearing the irritating noise of the man's groans, Walt felt his blood rushing to pound in his temples. Preparing to push Cory away and go after the man, the sound of Brock's voice stopped Walt from making the mistake he would have regretted later when he came to his senses.

Raising his voice above the sound of the siren, Brock stared at the sheriff holding

Cory. "Stay where you're at Walt."
With one look, Brock could see Cory was
dead and knew what had to be going
through Walt's mind.
"Let Kim and I handle this guy. Taking care
of Cory's body is your job now."

Drawing in a deep breath, Walt's body
shook with emotion as he exhaled. Glad for
Brock's interference, Walt nodded before
turning his attention back to the lifeless
body on his lap.

Seeing the ambulance turn into the station
parking lot, Brock wrenched the man's
elbow he held. The motion pulled the man
away from Kim as he dropped to his knees,
another scream echoing through the air.
Pulling the man up, Brock shook his head.
"C'mon Ortiz, your ride's here."
Brock turned to Kim. "I'll ride in the
ambulance, you follow in the SUV."

Kim nodded. "I'll be right behind you."

Half dragging the man, Brock headed for the
ambulance. Instead of heading for the SUV,
Kim dropped on the ground next to Walt.
"This isn't your fault. Brock and I should

have realized Daniel Ortiz would be watching Cory. I'm sorry Walt. This never should have happened. We have Ortiz and alive. We'll make him talk and then he'll pay for taking Cory's life. I promise you that."

Reaching out, Kim gently touched Walt's slumped shoulder. "I'm sorry Walt. I have to get to the hospital. I'll be back as soon as I can."
Unsure if Walt had heard her words, Kim stood and left the man to his grief. Before she headed for the vehicle, she ran into the station to make sure Lucy had called the coroner and then hurried out to the car and away from the horrific scene of the young man's unnecessary death.

Even though she'd lost sight of the ambulance, Kim had no problem finding the hospital. The larger building towered over and stood out from the other structures in the small town of Deer Valley.

Parking the SUV, Kim rushed into the hospital and found Brock pacing the floor of the waiting room.

Brock looked over at her, seeing the questions echoed in her brown eyes as Kim brushed her bangs away from them. He couldn't keep the anger out of his voice. "Ortiz is in surgery. They have to take the bullet out of his shoulder. He'll be sore and tired, but his vocal cords are working. As soon as he's stable we'll get him transferred to Helena. How's Walt?"

Kim shook her head. "I don't know. This isn't something he's going to be able to shake off. Damn it Brock. We should have known Ortiz would be waiting. What the hell were we thinking?"

Brock shook his head. "We weren't thinking. I have no excuses and we owe Walt big time. Right now, we have to try and put that aside. Don't forget Ortiz is our assignment. We make the bastard talk and get him moved, then we try and somehow make things right with Walt."

Although Kim knew the likelihood of making things better for Walt were slim, she nodded then sighed. "Do you think there's a coffee machine around this place?"

Brock shrugged. "Let's go find out."

Twenty minutes later, the two were seated back in the waiting room drinking bitter coffee. Brock took time to text Aaron to explain the situation, promising to keep his boss apprised of the situation.

After Brock was finished, Kim shook her head and grimaced as she sipped her drink. "It's bad enough to be in this place, you'd think they could have a decent cup of coffee available."

Turning to Kim, Brock grinned. "I've had worse. Blame it on the atmosphere. I just wish they'd hurry up. I told the doctor Ortiz was under arrest and I wanted to not only talk to him but that he was to have a guard on his room. The doctors' name is Prescott." Brock frowned. "Do you have Ortiz's gun and phone? I lost track of everything getting him in the ambulance? We need to get those things to FBI headquarters in Helena."

Brock's partner nodded. "It's okay, they're locked in the SUV."
Kim sighed and looked at her watch. "You know, we haven't really been here that long,

it just feels like forever. This whole thing has got to be a hell of a lot worse for Walt. I wish we would have moved Cory the minute we arrived."

Brock shook his head. "No guarantees, no matter what we would have done. Stop beating yourself up over this Kim. The best way to honor Cory is to stop whoever is behind the bomb threats."

Kim frowned. "It's damn strange an illegal immigrant from Haiti is listed as working at the President's resort. You know what he said about people from Haiti."

Brock grunted. "Among other countries. The President hates minorities unless he can get them to work for him for nothing."

Kim laughed. "Good thing I'm the only one to hear you say that. I can just imagine the twitter rant that would put the President on."

Brock half choked on the drink of coffee he was taking. Before he could answer, a doctor stepped in the room.

"Agent Odom, your prisoner is out of surgery. He's in the recovery room."

Brock stood quickly and the doctor shook
his head. "Don't worry, he's still under the
anesthetic. The nurses have orders to move
him the moment he begins waking up. I'll
show you to the room where they'll be
taking him. We removed the bullet from Mr.
Ortiz's shoulder. He lost quite a bit of blood,
but he'll make a full recovery."

Kim stood beside Brock. "When can we talk
to him?"

Looking at Kim, the doctor frowned. Seeing
the look, Brock smiled. "I'm sorry doctor,
This is my partner, Agent Mackey."

Doctor Prescott nodded his greeting.
"I'd say within an hour, you can question
Mr. Ortiz. I know he's your prisoner, but, as
a doctor, I have to limit your questioning to
fifteen minutes for now. He is still my
patient."

Brock nodded. "We understand, but you
should know that our ability to question Mr.
Ortiz is a matter of great security to our
country. We can't explain why, but many
people are still in danger because of the man
who is your patient."

Staring at Brock and then Kim, the doctor could read the seriousness of the situation in their faces and nodded. "Let me take you to his room and I'll give you as much time as I can."

Doctor Prescott escorted the agents to an empty room and then left them to wait for the arrival of Daniel Ortiz. Kim walked over to the window and looked out. "I wish this room was on the second floor. I can just see Ortiz escaping out through this window."

Brock shook his head. "Not with us taking turns watching him. Once we get him in here we can question him. Then one of us can head back to the hotel while the other stays here. With just the two of us, we're going to have to take twelve hour shifts. Do you want day or night?"

Kim sighed. "I'll take days. I can't sleep in the daytime, never could. That is if it's okay with you. I have to warn you though, I can lose some beauty sleep but not much."

The laugh echoed in the room as Brock shook his head. "You don't have any worries in that area, but you can take the day shift. I don't have any problems sleeping in the day. I've always been lucky in that area. I can sleep any place and any time."

The sound of Brock's phone ringing had both the agents jumping startled. Pulling out his phone, Brock looked at Kim.
"It's Aaron."

Taking a seat, Kim focused on the one sided conversation. She knew Brock wouldn't want to put Aaron on speaker phone in case anyone entered the room.

Lifting the phone to his ear, Brock sighed. "Aaron, I'm glad you called back, but you should know that they haven't brought Ortiz back from recovery yet."

In his office, Aaron had removed his tie and was leaned back in his seat after a rough day. "That's okay, you can update me on Ortiz later. I wanted to bring you up to date. We finally arranged to get into the Many Lakes Resort and found the bomb. I'm guessing neither you or Kim has watched the news lately."

Green eyes narrowing, Brock shook his head. "What's going on now?"

Aaron let out a groan. "Actually nothing we shouldn't have expected. The President was busy on his twitter account talking about the FBI's lack of skill. After that, he made a short statement to the press expressing his dismay that our agents are trying to set him up. He says our arriving at both of his resorts is a scheme against him. He accused the FBI of using the bomb scare to get in the buildings and plant fake evidence that would show either he is working with Russia or trying to stop any investigations. If the President can show the FBI and other intelligence agencies are inept, he can use that when any evidence is unearthed by the committees looking into him. Now that the bomb in Florida is no longer a problem, I really need you to get some answers from Ortiz. We need to get that resort in Helena checked over. The President still has the groundbreaking ceremony set for the ninth. I'm not even going to try and draw a conclusion about who hired Ortiz right now, but the fact he worked at one of the President's resorts links the two in ways I hate to even consider."

Brock nodded. "We'll get him to talk. When
Ortiz is stable I want to move him to Helena
where the other agents are. Kim and I want
to be at that resort when the President gets
there. If Ortiz has to stay in the hospital,
we'll keep him guarded and as soon as he
can be released from medical care, he can be
transferred to the jail there. I'm sure it's a
bigger and more secure facility than the one
here in Deer Valley."

A frown creased Aaron's forehead. "Are the
two of you okay guarding Ortiz or do you
want me to send someone to help?"

Glancing over at Kim, Brock grinned. "The
two of us are doing just fine. I'll let you
know when we're headed to Helena."

Brock hung up the phone and quickly
explained to Kim what had happened with
the investigation and the President's
backlash. Just as he was finishing, a male
nurse pushed a bed into the room. Kim and
Brock watched the man maneuver the bed
with its' occupant into the space in the
center of the room. When he was finished,
the nurse checked first the IV running into
Daniel Ortiz's arm and then took a few

moments to check the man's vitals before looking over at Kim and Brock.

"Mr. Ortiz is still coming out of sedation. Doctor Prescott will be here in a moment. He asked that you not question the patient until he arrives."

The nurse waited for the agents to nod before he left them alone in the room with Daniel Ortiz.

Standing, Kim stretched before moving closer to the bed in order to get a better look at the patient who was also their prisoner. She stood five feet back and stared at Daniel Ortiz. Instead of being what you would call pale, Kim thought the man's skin had a gray undertone to it. She imagined he had lost a lot of blood. Other than the bandage that ran from the man's chest over his shoulder, Daniel Ortiz just looked like a man sleeping. With no visible bruises, at least the man couldn't come back hollering abuse by the agents.

Brock stood next to Kim and pointed toward Daniel Ortiz. "Hell, I feel a lot worse than that guy looks."

Before Kim could answer, the doctor
stepped in the door. He glanced at the
agents, but moved to the bed without
speaking to them. Touching the shoulder
that was without a bandage, the doctor spoke
in a tone slightly louder than normal.
"Mr. Ortiz, Daniel, you're in the hospital.
You've had surgery. I removed a bullet from
your shoulder. Daniel, can you hear me?"

On the bed, Daniel turned his head slightly
toward the voice and nodded slowly. The
voice came out haltingly and with a fairly
thick accent. "I can hear you. Tired, really
tired."

The doctor nodded. "That's normal. I need
to inform you that two FBI agents are here
to speak with you. I'm going to let them ask
a few questions. Anytime you feel you are
too tired to answer, let me know."
Doctor Prescott stepped back from the bed a
couple of steps and turned to the agents, a
look of warning in the blue eyes.

Looking back at the man, Brock also held a
similar look in his green eyes. He wasn't
worried about Ortiz's health, other than
needing the man to remain stable until they

got answers out of him. "When will he be ready to be moved?"

The doctor frowned. "The man just had surgery. I know he is a criminal, but for me, he is a patient first."

Not wanting Brock to end up on the doctor's bad side, Kim moved forward a step. "What agent Odom means is we'd like to have Mr. Ortiz moved to Helena as soon as possible."

The doctor shrugged. "Barring any setbacks, I think you are looking at a day, maybe two for that."

Giving the doctor a smile, Kim nodded. "Thank you. We promise to go slow." As she spoke, Kim turned to Brock, her brown eyes narrowing in a warning look.

Nodding at her, Brock turned back to the doctor. "Agent Mackey is right. I'm sorry if I sounded harsh."

Nodding, the doctor took another step back and watched the agents move to the foot of Daniel Ortiz's bed.

Brock raised his voice slightly, echoing what the doctor had done. "I'm Agent Odom

and this is Agent Mackey, we met earlier. Daniel Ortiz, you are under arrest for the murder of Cory Baxter and for several bomb threats, including those against Federal agencies. I read your rights to you in the ambulance, but am going to repeat them so there is no misunderstanding. Please nod if you understand."
Brock waited for the slight nod from the man on the bed, then quoted the rights he had memorized years ago.
When he finished, Brock moved so he was leaning over the foot of the hospital bed.
"Who paid you to come after and shoot Cory Baxter today?"

The head full of dark hair shook back and forth against the white pillow. "Accident, it was an a accident."

Shaking his own head, Brock drew in a couple breaths to calm himself before continuing. "We both know that isn't true. You were shooting toward a police station in the daylight. We know you paid Cory Baxter to mail the letter with the bomb threats. We know you work at the Many Lakes resort in Florida making minimum wage, but drive a very expensive car. Who's paying you Daniel?"

Seeing the brown eyes open wide followed by rough shaking of his head, Kim grabbed the foot of the bed. "Daniel, please, we're here to help you. You must have family or maybe friends that work with you at the resort. Do you know the danger they were in? We almost didn't get to the bomb in time." Kim knew she was stretching the truth because the bomb was fake, but she was hoping Daniel Ortiz didn't know that.

Daniel frowned. "It wasn't a real bomb."

Surprised the man knew that, but determined to continue her bluff, Kim shook her head and sighed. "Your wrong Mister Ortiz, it was real. Our agents took it away and disarmed it. That bomb was definitely meant to not only explode, but was placed to do the most damage possible."
Knowing she was stating facts that weren't true, Kim only hoped her story was convincing to the man on the hospital bed. She knew the bombs found so far weren't armed, but that didn't necessarily mean the rest of the bombs were also fake.

Again, Daniel's head shook vehemently, but Kim noticed an underlying worried and nervous look in the dark eyes as Daniel spoke. "I don't know nothin' about that." After speaking that sentence to the agents, Daniel turned to the doctor. "I'm really tired. I don't think I can handle any more questioning right now."

Doctor Prescott nodded, although he knew Daniel should be feeling more energetic now that the anesthetic was wearing off.
"It's your decision, you know how you feel better than we do."
The doctor turned to the agents. "I'm going to have to ask you both to leave, the patient needs to get some rest."

Brock grunted slightly, but nodded.
"Of course, I just want you and Daniel to know that either Agent Mackey or myself will be right outside the door. Mister Ortiz is still under arrest. If he hadn't been shot, he'd be in a jail cell right now instead of a hospital bed. I hope both of you will keep that in mind."

Leaving the room, Brock and Kim waited in the hallway outside the door. A few minutes later, Doctor Prescott stepped out, leaving the room door open a few inches.

Staring at the man, Brock was frowning. "Can the window in that room be opened?"

The doctor shook his head. "No, we have safety windows in place in case a patient has mental disabilities. Their safety is always our number one priority. I suppose an ambitious person might find a way to throw a chair out or something, but I have never seen that or heard of it happening."

Thinking about the possibility, Brock finally nodded. With either him or Kim outside the door, he didn't think Daniel would try to escape. If he did, they should be able to hear him. "Alright, thank you doctor. I hope you realize that we will be guarding this door until Daniel can be moved to the hospital in Helena or the jail when he is well enough."

The doctor nodded. "I understand. I hope you realize I took an oath, as I know you did. My job is to help people and there is the confidentiality between a patient and their doctor to be thought of. I also realize why you want to get Daniel Ortiz to jail as soon

as possible. I didn't know about the bomb
threats, but I knew Cory Baxter was killed.
Deer Valley is a small town, everyone knew
Cory. His death is a deep loss."
Doctor Prescott frowned. "Why don't we get
the two of you some chairs? They won't be
as comfortable as you might hope for, but
they should help make your waiting easier."

Brock nodded and turned to Kim. "I'll go
with the doctor, you wait hear and listen."

Leaning against the wall, Kim folded her
arms across her chest while she waited the
ten minutes it took before the two men came
back, each carrying a chair.
Once the chairs were placed next to the
hospital room door, the doctor left. Brock
and Kim sat down.

Turning to Brock, Kim frowned, her brown
eyes looking tired. "Neither of us has eaten.
Why don't I run to the cafeteria and get us
some dinner?"

A smile lit up Brock's face. "That sounds
great. After we eat, I need you to go talk to
Walt. I didn't see Daniel's car, but it must
be parked close to the station. I need Walt to

have it impounded. We need to call the FBI office in Helena and get some people from the forensics office here to process the vehicle. When they show up, you can give them the phone and gun we took from Daniel.”

Kim nodded. “I’ll take care of it, but dinner first.”

Brock nodded, the grin never leaving his face.

Within an hour, the two finished their dinner, which both had to admit was better than expected, especially after the bad coffee earlier.

Brock carried their trays to the nurses station sitting thirty feet away and then returned to see Kim slumping back in her seat and covering a yawn. Brock tried to hide the grin that covered his face but without much luck. “Kim, go on and get out of here. You still have a stop before you can get to bed.”

Kim nodded. “Guess I better.”
A frown appeared as her brown eyes darkened. “Have you thought about the investigation into your shooting Daniel?

What if you're put on suspension while it is
looked into?"

Brock shook his head. "I think Aaron can
take care of that. I know there will be one,
but Aaron can make sure it is put on hold.
I'll talk to him about it. I need to call him
and get him up to speed on what's been
happening. There's no way I'm stopping
now. We're too damn close."
Waving a hand toward the hospital room
door, Brock shook his head. His voice was
raw as he spoke. "Daniel Ortiz is not getting
away with Cory's death."

Kim nodded. "I was hoping you'd say that."
Standing up, Kim placed a hand on Brock's
shoulder. "Now, when I get to the motel, I'll
sleep better."

Watching Kim walk away, Brock gave silent
thanks that he'd been partnered with her. He
liked working with his partner James Long,
but had come to respect Kim in the short
time they had been working together.
Moving to the door, Brock looked inside at a
sleeping Daniel before he again took his seat
and prepared for a long night.

Chapter 7

Two hours later, Kim was pulling in behind the police station. She was certain Walt had gone home, but she didn't have his personal phone number. Taking Daniel's phone and gun with her, Kim headed inside. She felt the items would be safer under lock and key at the station until someone from the FBI office in Helena could get to Deer Valley and take them into their possession.

Stepping in the police station, Kim was relieved to see a face she recognized behind the front desk.

A smile covered the man's face as he looked up. "Agent Mackey, how are you?"

Kim shrugged. "Hello Deputy Carlyle. As good as can be expected I guess and the name is Kim."

Deputy Carlyle smiled. "Good to hear and you can call me Brian."

Moving over to the desk, Kim pulled out a chair and sat down before speaking. "Thanks Brian. I don't suppose the sheriff is around? I really need to talk to him."

Shaking his head, Brian sighed. "He's not. Walt's really been having a hard time. He had to take care of things at the coroner's office. He came back here for a while, but said he was heading to Cory's house. I'm guessing he's still there. Do you want me to give his cell a call and make sure?"

Kim nodded. "I'd appreciate that and could you ask him if I could meet him there? I also need to put a call in to the FBI office in Helena. I don't have their number either."

The deputy nodded. "Let me call Walt and then I'll get that for you."

Sitting in the chair, Kim waited for Brian to okay her visit with Walt and then as he found the FBI number for her. As soon as Brian found the number he wrote it down and handed Kim the phone.

As soon as the connection was made, Kim gave her name, the district agency she worked for, her badge number and then

Aaron Jackson's name. Once that was finished she explained to the FBI operator what she needed to help with the investigation. Kim wasn't surprised to find the FBI office had been expecting her call and had already talked with Aaron. When the call was over, Kim asked Brian to lock up Daniel Ortiz's phone and handgun. The first half of her assignment done, Kim went in search of Walt, knowing the second part of her job tonight was going to be the hardest. It wasn't worrying about Walt impounding Daniel Ortiz's car, but facing Walt after Cory's untimely and unwarranted death that Kim knew was going to be hard.

Retracing the route Brock had driven earlier, Kim easily found her way to Cory's house and pulled into the gravel driveway behind Walt's police car. She sat in the car a moment gathering her thoughts before finally opening the car door and heading to the house.

Before she reached the front door, Walt opened it. "Hi Kim, any luck with Ortiz?"

Kim shook her head. "He hasn't said much. Brock is spending the night at the hospital. I relieve him in the morning. Hopefully by then Daniel will be stable enough to move. If we can't get him to talk, the agents at the headquarters in Helena will."

Walt nodded. "Come on in. I came back here to lock up and then decided to straighten Cory's house."
Walt grunted. "Don't ask me why."

Following behind Walt, Kim felt her heart aching for the man. She shrugged. "The reasons don't matter. It's just something you felt you needed to do and that's motivation enough."

In the living room, Walt pointed toward the couch. "Have a seat. Do you want a drink? Cory has some sodas in the fridge."

Kim shook her head as she heard the way Walt stumbled over saying the word has. She imagined using words with present and past tense would be something Walt was going to have a hard time with for quite some time. "I'm okay. But thanks. I want to tell you again how sorry I am about Cory. I know he was special to you. I've seen a lot of senseless deaths, but it never gets easier."

Staring at Kim, Walt could hear the sincerity in her voice and nodded. "I grew up with Cory's parents. After they died, I tried to watch out for him."

Kim frowned. "Don't blame yourself Walt. None of us thought Daniel Ortiz would be waiting for Cory already. The whole thing is a damn shame."

Walt nodded. "Thanks for saying that. You didn't come here to talk about Cory though, what did you need?"

Kim sighed, hating to bother the sheriff with Cory's death on his mind. Hoping that keeping busy might help, she nodded. "Brock asked me to see if you would look for Daniel Ortiz's car. If he was driving the one Cory described, it shouldn't be hard to find. We need to get that vehicle impounded so a search can be done. You never know what little piece of evidence will end up assisting the investigation."

Walt nodded. "I'll take care of it myself. I'm done here. I just need to lock up. If you and Brock are still around, Cory's funeral will be on the seventh."

Kim frowned. "We'll try and make it. I think we'll still be in Helena. Remember the bomb at Treasure Hill resort isn't supposed to go off until the ninth, the same day the President is holding that ridiculous opening ceremony. I know Aaron will want us around to keep a watch on the place."

Walt stood. "You look tired. Let's lock up and you can head back to your motel. I'll get that car impounded. I'll check in with you or Brock at the hospital in the morning."

Getting to her feet, Kim put out her hand. When Walt took it, she gripped his large hand as tight as she could. "Thanks for your help. I want you to know that I think Cory really was a good kid. He helped us a lot giving us Daniel Ortiz's name."

Walt smiled. "Thanks Kim, I appreciate your saying that. You're right, Cory had some bad habits, but inside he was a good person."
Letting go of Kim's hand, Walt drew in a deep breath and let it out slowly. "Let's get out of here."

After Walt locked up, Kim went to her car
and backed out of the driveway. As she
drove back to the hotel she felt better about
Walt. He was upset over Cory's death, but
she didn't see the anger against Daniel Ortiz
she worried he would be holding.
Kim's admiration of the man went up a
notch.

While Kim was driving to the motel for a
night's sleep. Brock was sitting in the
hospital with a Styrofoam cup of coffee in
his hand. He was grateful to the nurses who
had taken pity on him and brought him the
hot beverage.

At the moment, one of those nurses was in
checking on Daniel Ortiz. In his chair,
Brock leaned toward the halfway open door
and struggled to listen in. Daniel was awake
and talking to the nurse. His voice was quiet,

but Brock could easily make out the words as Daniel inquired about making a phone call. The nurse must have handed Daniel the room phone because Brock could hear her telling Daniel how to get an outside line before she excused herself to let him have privacy.

The nurse stepped out into the hall and smiled at Brock. "Do you need a refill on that coffee?"

Brock shook his head. "Not right now. I really appreciate the offer though. Everyone at the Hospital has been so helpful."

Smiling at the compliment the nurse headed down the hallway. Brock stood, leaned against the door frame and listened in.

He could only hear one side of the conversation but was able to get the essence of what was being talked about as he heard Daniel's voice.

"I told you, I'm in big trouble here. With Cory Baxter dead the FBI is charging me with whatever they can think of. You talked me into this. I want a lawyer up here and pronto. Talk to the damn boss. When you do, remind him that I know what the bodies are buried."

Daniel was silent a moment. Brock knew whoever was on the other end of the line was answering his request. A few seconds later, Daniel's voice sounded again, a bit louder than before. "You're damn right you'll take care of it. If you're not in Helena by the time they move me, you can bet your ass I will be spilling my guts."

Brock heard the phone being slammed down. Lifting his wrist, Brock stared at his watch until a minute ticked slowly by and then he pushed the door open.

"What's going on in here Daniel? I thought I heard you yelling."

Daniel shook his head as he reached over and placed the phone on the bedside table. "Nothing's going on. I was just making the phone call I am entitled to by law. I guess that slipped your mind. One other right I decided to use, is the right to remain silent. I'm not saying anything else until my lawyer gets here."

Brock shrugged. "Suit yourself Daniel. I'd
never refuse you your rights. Just keep a
couple things in mind. You are not actually
a citizen of this country and you are facing
some heavy charges that only begin with
murder."

Not waiting for a response, Brock turned
and walked out the door, his eyes dancing
with humor. He hoped his warning would
bounce around in Daniel's' mind and eat at
his nerves while he waited to be moved to
Helena and for his lawyer to make an
appearance.

Once in the hall, Brock took his seat, now
more awake than he had been, as he waited
for the morning and Kim to come around.

Chapter 8

Although Kim had set the alarm on her watch, she was up hours before it was set to go off. Getting out of bed, Kim only took the time for a quick shower before heading to the hospital.

Walking down the hall, she frowned seeing Walt standing with Brock outside Daniel's door. Kim had expected the sheriff to visit, but Walt had to have been up before the sun. That was if he had even slept. Kim had an idea if Walt had bothered to try, his sleep would have been restless, at best.

Replacing the frown with a smile, Kim greeted the men. "Good morning Brock, thanks for taking the night shift."
She turned to the sheriff. "It's good to see you Walt."

Both men nodded and returned the greeting, but it was Brock who took the job of filling Kim in on the overnight developments.
"I have good news and bad news. First, the

good news. Walt's been busy. He's impounded Daniel's vehicle. If you can believe it, he was actually driving that BMW. Guess he wasn't trying to be inconspicuous. Anyway, Helena is sending a team here. They'll be going over that car with a fine tooth comb. Now, the bad news. Daniel made a late night call. A lawyer is on his way. I was able to catch Daniel's side of the conversation. He wasn't very happy about his situation and let his caller know that in no uncertain terms. One thing he said really caught my attention though. He told whoever was on the other end of the line to tell the boss he knew where the bodies were buried. I think Daniel Ortiz has some secrets we need to know."

Shaking her head, Kim sighed. "Yeah, but will he spill anything with a lawyer around?"

Brock shrugged. "The way I see it, Daniel's in some serious trouble. For starters, he's an illegal immigrant. Then add in bomb threats and murder. I might be wrong, but when you're looking at the death penalty, it loosens tongues."

Kim frowned. "I hope you're right. I guess we'll find out soon enough. For now, all that can wait. Why don't I take over your job here and let you head to the motel and get some rest?"

Brock shook his head. "I could use some sleep, but I want to wait to see what the doctor has to say. He's supposed to be making his rounds this morning. I'm hoping he'll release Daniel and let us move him. I'd feel a lot better with him in Helena." Brock sighed. "Even if he's in the hospital instead of a jail cell. The FBI is in the capital and we still have that last bomb threat. The agents still haven't found the bomb. I don't know why the secret service hasn't talked the President out of that big ceremony scheduled for the ninth. Then again, you know how the President likes attention. The secret service is aware that's the same day that bomb is set to go off."

Listening to Brock, Walt ignored the talk of the bomb threat, thinking instead of what Brock said about moving Ortiz.
Walt smiled. "I happen to know the jail in

Helena has a great infirmary. I think they're equipped to take care of a gunshot wound."

Both Kim and Brock felt their hopes soar with Walt's words. Transferring Daniel straight to the jail would save a lot of hassle. It would also free both of them to be at Treasure Hill Resort on the ninth.

Turning to Brock, Kim frowned. "If you aren't going to the motel, how about I grab us some coffee?"

Lifting his leg and stretching it, Brock repeated the motion with the other leg and laughed. "Let me grab the coffee. I've been sitting in that damn chair all night. I'm as stiff as a board. I'll grab us all a cup and hopefully get back before the doctor shows up."

Walt shook his head. "None for me. I'm heading to the station. I have no desire to see Daniel Ortiz. To tell you the truth, I don't trust myself not to shoot the bastard, I'd appreciate it if you kept me informed on what happens with Cory's killer though."

Placing a hand on Walt's shoulder, Brock let out a sigh and nodded. "We've all felt the same way you are Walt. Don't worry, we'll keep contact."

Her brown eyes glistening, Kim also nodded. "You'll know anything the minute we do. Thanks for all your help. I'm just so sorry it turned out like this. Brock and I liked Cory too."
Even as she said the words, Kim knew they were inadequate. She had no idea what she could say that could help though.

After the goodbyes were said, Kim watched Brock and Walt walk away, with Brock headed to the cafeteria and Walt headed back to the jail. She shook her head at the awfulness of the situation and took a seat in one of the chairs sitting in front of the hospital room door. She could have went in the room and checked on Daniel, but after talking to Walt, she didn't want to look at the man either.

Looking down the hall, Kim saw the doctor headed toward her and was relieved when he turned into a room a few doors down from Daniel Ortiz's. Kim hoped that meant the doctor had to check on a couple of patients before he came to see Daniel Ortiz. She sighed, hoping Brock would be back before that happened.

Pulling out her phone, Kim thought about texting an update to her husband and then decided to wait until they heard what the doctor had to say. Slipping the phone back in her pocket, Kim stood and paced the hall until she saw Brock headed toward her.

Holding a tray in front of him, Brock smiled at Kim as he got closer. "I hope you appreciate what a great guy I am. Not only did I bring coffee, but I got you a ham and cheese croissant."

Nodding, Kim laughed. "I'll be in debt to you forever. I was starving. Thanks Brock."

Sitting down, the two ate their breakfast. Kim was taking the tray to the nurse's station when Doctor Prescott headed past her to Daniel's room. She turned and began walking back just as Brock stood up. "Doctor Prescott, I'm glad you're here. I'm hoping you'll be able to tell us that Daniel is stable enough to move. The sheriff informed Kim and I that the jail in Helena has a great infirmary. I'd rather have him moved there than to a hospital."

The doctor shrugged. "I'll have to do my exam before I can confirm anything. I know you'd rather have Daniel in jail, but like I told you before, I have to put my personal feelings aside. My profession is something I take seriously."

Brock nodded. "Of course, I didn't mean to imply anything different. I just wanted to tell you about the option that has come up."

The doctor nodded and pushed open Daniel's door. Just as he was stepping in, Brock stopped him. "Is it okay if Kim and I come in while you do your examination?"

Turning back, the doctor nodded. "I wouldn't have it any other way. Let's go see how the patient is feeling."

It took twenty minutes for the doctor to examine Daniel. Kim and Brock stood at the foot of the bed. Although both of them were anxious, they kept their faces set with no emotion showing. When the doctor finished, he pointed toward the hallway.

Following Kim and Brock out into the hall, Doctor Prescott looked at both agents, but addressed his words more to Brock. "You can move Daniel. He is stable enough for an ambulance ride and the transfer to the jail in Helena. Luckily the bullet passed all the way through Daniel's shoulder. He has some damage, but nothing that can't be taken care of by the doctor's at the jail infirmary."

Kim and Brock both smiled at the doctors' words. Brock put out his hand, which the doctor grabbed. Shaking the man's hand, Brock nodded. "I can't thank you enough. I know this decision is a hard one to make."

Letting go of Brock's hand, the doctor shrugged. "It wasn't a hard decision. Medically, I know Daniel is stable. I want you to know I'm glad that was what I found. Like I told you before, Cory Baxter had some problems but he was a good kid. I need to fill out the paperwork for the transfer, but you should be able to get out of here in a couple hours,"

After the doctor walked away, Brock smiled at Kim. "Looks like our lucky day. With two hours to wait, I think I will head to the motel and take a shower. I'll pack up my clothes while I'm there. I want to ride in the ambulance with Daniel. I hope you won't mind driving the car and following us."

Kim shook her head. "I don't mind, in fact I was going to ask you if I could. Right now, I don't think I could spend any time with Daniel Ortiz. I keep seeing Walt's face."

Brock nodded. "I know what you mean. Hopefully we can get some information from Daniel and still make him pay for what he did to Cory."

Kim sighed. "I just hope his lawyer doesn't try to stop any of that."

Giving his agreement with Kim's sentiment, Brock left the hospital.

Taking her seat, Kim glanced at the door that led to Daniel Ortiz's room. Not wanting to even think about the man for now, she instead pulled out her cell phone. Knowing her husband would be at work and not answering calls, Kim texted him an update. She took time to let Blake know she would be heading to Helena with not only her new

partner but with Daniel in custody.
Frowning at the text, Kim's heart ached to be back home with Blake. She added an "I love and miss you" to the end of the text before sending. Still holding the phone, Kim still felt empty and added another text to the first. "I looking forward to getting home and think it may be time for an extended vacation." Kim decided to add one more line. "Love you forever." And then sent the text.

Knowing she wouldn't be getting an answer right away, Kim tucked her phone in her pocket. A few minutes later she frowned with curiosity at the sound of her phone's ding that meant a text had come in. Pulling her phone from her pocket, Kim smiled at Blake's return text.
"Love you forever too."

Kim leaned back in her chair, head resting against the wall and waited. The sound of someone walking toward her had Kim sitting up and watching a nurse head toward the door to Daniel's room.
The woman smiled at Kim. "Doctor Prescott just informed me we are losing Mister Ortiz

as a patient. I'll be the one getting him ready for the trip."
Looking around, the nurse frowned. "Did Brock leave?"

Kim nodded. "He just ran to get a shower and change. He should be back shortly. I wouldn't want to move Daniel out of here without his help."

The nurse smiled and nodded. "I had a few conversations with Brock overnight. He certainly seems to be capable and those green eyes of his are amazing."

Staring at the nurse's face, Kim smiled. It looked like Brock had made quite an impression on her. Kim thought of Brock as a partner and hadn't paid much attention to his green eyes, but she could see the woman in front of her must have.
Kim nodded. "I'm sure Brock would be glad to hear you noticed those eyes of his. He should be back well before the doctor finishes the paperwork on Daniel. Maybe you two can get another chance to talk before we leave."

The smile broadened as the nurse nodded and then headed into the door to prepare Daniel for transfer.

Kim shook her head in astonishment once the nurse was gone. She couldn't help but wonder if women like the one she had just talked to were part of the reason Brock Odom was still single. Sort of like the so many women so little time, idea.
With Brock first and foremost in her mind, Kim was surprised to see him walking down the hallway towards her.

As he stepped up, Brock stared at Kim. He couldn't quite place the look she was giving him. The humor in her brown eyes had him frowning. "What did I do now?"

Kim laughed. "Nothing really. I just didn't know you were such a charmer."
Kim pointed at the door. "The nurse who apparently was on duty last night is getting Daniel ready to be released for his transfer."
Kim smiled. "By the way, she seemed quite impressed with those green eyes of yours."

Brock laughed. "Well of course she is. Maybe I should walk in and see if she needs any help. Want to join me?"

Shaking her head, Kim held out her hand. "No thanks, but if you're done with the car keys, I'll take them back."

Reaching in his pocket, Brock handed Kim the keys. "Here you go. I tossed my things in the back of the SUV. You can grab yours from the hotel and then, if you don't mind, let the front desk know we are leaving."

Glad for something to do, Kim grabbed the keys and stood up, preparing to leave. Just as she made the motion, the sound of Daniel Ortiz's voice could be heard coming through the slightly opened door and he didn't sound happy.

"What the hell is wrong with you? I told you I'm in deep shit here. C'mon Adelman, yesterday you said you'd be flying right out to help."

The silence that followed let Brock and Kim know whoever Daniel had called was talking. When Daniel finally answered, his voice wasn't as loud. In fact, the tone almost was more like pleading.

"Rueben, you're the only person who can get me out of this. It sounds like you're just brushing me off. Who is Hal Ostrum? What law firm is he with? With the charges I'm looking at, I need you here."

Again silence, then Daniel raised his voice again. "If I don't like this guy or feel he's not doing me any good, I'm warning you, I have no problem cutting a deal and saving my ass."

Kim and Brock stared at each other, stunned. The two of them had heard the name Rueben Adelman before.
Kim started shaking her head in disbelief. "Daniel can't be talking to the Rueben Adelman we know about."

Brock shrugged. "I don't think it's a coincidence that Daniel worked at Many Lakes resort and Rueben Adelman works for the man that owns that place too. Except Adelman's job is in the White House."

The anger in Daniel's shouted voice and the words he spoke, let Kim and Brock know their suspicions were right.

"The hell with you Adelman. I don't care if it is my word against his. I'll make sure the FBI believes me. At the very least they'll check into the allegations."

A slamming sound was followed by the nurse hurrying out of the room. The worried look on her face turned into a smile when she saw Brock. Ignoring Kim, the nurse moved closer to her partner.

Brock smiled back at her and pointed toward Daniel's door. "Hi Gina, sounds like you're earning your money today."

Gina sighed. "Sounds to me like Mr. Ortiz has some friends in high places."
The blue eyes frowned. "Or maybe I should say he did have. The way he hung up that phone, I don't think Daniel Ortiz and Rueben Adelman have much of a relationship now."

Brock nodded. "Sorry you had to listen to that. Is Daniel all ready to be moved?"

Gina shrugged. "Other than the doctor signing Mister Ortiz's release paper. Why don't I go and see if he has it ready?"
Gina didn't wait for an answer as she turned and hurried down the hall.

Ten minutes later, it was Doctor Prescott instead of Gina who returned carrying papers in his hand. He frowned at Kim and Brock. "By the way Gina was acting, I think it's a good thing Daniel Ortiz is being moved out of this hospital."
The doctor handed Brock the papers.
"You'll find Daniel's release in there, along with my orders for what he will be needing for his medical care. I've called the prison in Helena and explained all that, but a paper trail helps to keep everyone on task. The ambulance is ready and waiting outside the back doors. If you're ready, let's go move your prisoner."

Nodding at the doctor, Brock then turned to Kim. "I can handle Ortiz. Why don't you go finish up at the motel? I'll make sure we take our time loading Daniel and wait for you to get back. That way you can follow us to the prison in Helena."

Glad to be in charge of driving the SUV instead of riding with Daniel Ortiz in the ambulance, Kim nodded and quickly left the hospital.

Chapter 9

Just over an hour later, Kim was driving the rented SUV and following behind the ambulance. Although glad for some time alone to clear her mind, Kim was also hating the interim that gave her mind free reign to twist and turn. Her earlier text to Blake was the main thing on her thoughts. In the years she'd been an agent she had never lost a witness before. She'd had close calls several times, but the guilt of Cory's death was a weight on her heart and mind. One she didn't like having there.

Although Kim had never wanted to have any other career other than being an FBI agent, she knew this assignment would be her last for an extended period of time. It wasn't just Cory's death that was bothering her. The fact that the President of the United States was doing everything he could to undermine the FBI and other agencies made all of their jobs harder. Kim hoped the investigation into the President would end soon. No matter the outcome, maybe then he would stop the tweeting and complaining about the job the agencies did. Kim could only hope the damage inflicted could be repaired. When she had first read the letter from the bomber, she had actually thought he had the same idea. Now, with the name of Rueben Adelman thrown into the mix, Kim was more certain than ever that herself and the rest of the FBI were on the wild goose chase she had mentioned before.

Despite her fears and worries, Kim smiled, thinking about the time she would be spending with Blake. Maybe he could take a few days off also. If not, it didn't matter, because she would be home and waiting for him when he finished his shift. That time together would be more than they had had in the last few years.

Feeling better, Kim stared ahead at the back of the ambulance in front of her. She wondered if Brock was having an easier time dealing with the assignment now that he had Daniel to talk to and acquire information from.

Ahead of Kim, inside the ambulance, Brock wasn't having any luck at all. Despite the fact, Daniel must have had a falling out with his lawyer, he still wasn't talking. He wouldn't even answer questions that had nothing to do with the bombs or the killing.

Brock had tried instigating conversation by asking Daniel if he missed Haiti. When he only received a stone cold glare, Brock had tried several more topics. Each had ended with the same conclusion. The EMT, riding in the back and monitoring Daniel, wasn't much for conversation either.
Tired of trying to talk to either, Brock shook his head. Pulling out his handcuffs, Brock cuffed Daniel's uninjured arm to the frame on the gurney he was being transferred on. He smiled as he locked Daniel down.
"It's not that I don't trust you, but I don't. I'm going to shut my eyes until we reach Helena and right now I don't have the patience to deal with any nonsense. Cuffing you makes that a lot easier."

Sitting on the hard bench seat, Brock tried to get comfortable. Finding that impossible,

Brock folded his hands over his chest and with a groan of displeasure closed his eyes.

To Brock, the feel of the EMT shaking his shoulder seemed to come only seconds after he closed his eyes.
"Agent Odom, we're pulling into the prison. You better wake up."

Sitting up, Brock nodded. "Thanks. I must have been more tired than I thought."

Feeling the ambulance slow and then stop, Brock released the handcuff from the gurney frame. With Daniel's bad shoulder and arm in a sling, Brock knew there was no possible way he could handcuff the man's hands together. Instead, he slipped the handcuff around his own wrist and locked it. The clicking sound seemed to reverberate inside the back of the ambulance. Brock tugged slightly, forcing Daniel's hand to fall off his lap. "Time to go Daniel."

Giving Brock a glare, Daniel sat up and slid off the gurney to a standing position. "I'm sure the EMT's are supposed to wheel me inside the jail on that thing. What'd ya do, forget I'm a wounded man? I'm still in a lot of pain here."

Brock grunted out a laugh. He was sure Daniel wasn't in as much agony as he was trying to convey. "I'm sure the booking won't take long. Then you can get back into a bed like you want. Just don't forget the infirmary is part of the prison."

The two stepped out of the ambulance as soon as the EMT pushed open the back doors. Kim was already standing and waiting for them. When she looked at Daniel, he leaned his bad shoulder slightly forward and grimaced.
Ignoring the phony display, Kim turned instead to Brock. "Let's get him inside and get this over with. I want to head to the FBI office and see if there have been any developments."

Nodding at Kim, Brock pulled Daniel by the handcuff that linked them and headed into the jail. Inside, two deputies were waiting for them, ready to take Daniel into custody. Both men, dressed in identical uniforms, paced in front of a tall desk. Brock was surprised to find the two had the paperwork in order and waiting for one of the agents to add their signature. Brock took the initiative and then watched Daniel get fingerprinted before he was escorted away.

Turning, Brock stared at Kim. "That went a million times better than I expected. Looks like we can get out of here."

"Not so fast."

Both agents turned at the sound of a familiar voice. Kim was the first to speak, her brown eyes wide. "Aaron, what in the world are you doing here? Who's holding things together in Washington?"

The sound of Aaron's laughter filled the area. "The guys in Washington can handle things out there. I was more worried about who would be babysitting the two of you. I thought about it and decided I was the best man for the job."

Aaron looked around at the several cops in the jail staring at the three of them.

He turned back to face Kim and Brock. "Why don't we go outside and talk? I can fill you in on my side of things and the two of you can do the same."

Brock and Kim followed Aaron out the back door of the jail to the parking lot. Once outside, Aaron shook his head. "Sorry to rush you out of there, but I don't think the local cops are too impressed with the FBI trying to take charge. For the most part, Daniel Ortiz is their problem now. Lord knows we have enough of our own."

Brushing her hands through her short blonde hair, Kim frowned. "I didn't realize we were a problem. The people in the jail seemed more than helpful to me."

Aaron nodded. "That's because the sooner they booked Daniel, the quicker they got the two of you out of the hair. Never mind about that. The first thing I want to do is get your vehicle back to the rental agency. No sense paying for one when the FBI has several at your disposal. Once we get that done, I'll drive all of us to the FBI headquarters. We have a few new twists and turns in the investigation."

Aaron looked at his watch. "I want the two of you back here at six. That's when a meeting has been set up for Ortiz to meet with his lawyer. I don't know much about him. Some guy named Hal Ostrum. Because Ortiz is in the infirmary, I'm told the jail has a special visiting room that has an audio link. You'll be able to hear whatever is said from the conference room in the jail."

The green eyes staring at Aaron frowned before Brock shrugged. "Sounds good, but this new guy is only there because Rueben Adelman pretty much threw Daniel Ortiz under the bus. I'd like to know why. What about you, what will you be doing while we listen in?"

Aaron smiled. "I'll be joining you. I wouldn't miss that for the world. It seems strange to me that Adelman bailed on Ortiz. We'll figure that out soon enough. First things first. Do you think you can find the rental agency on your GPS or do you just want to follow me?"

Brock laughed. "I'll follow you. I don't trust GPS."

Kim nodded. "I'm with Brock on that one. I've heard horror stories about those things."

Looking at both agents, Aaron shook his head in disbelief. "And here I was thinking the two of you were technology geeks."

Laughing, Kim shook her head. "Only on some things. You know, the tried and tested technology that's got all the bugs out."

Aaron smiled. "Have it your way. Let's get going, the rest of the team at the FBI building are waiting to meet you two."

Within an hour, the rental car was returned. Brock and Kim had ridden with Aaron to the FBI building. Now, the three had just walked into a large conference room where four people were seated at a large table. A man with dark hair and eyes stood and motioned at the three. "Agent Jackson, glad you're back and with your team. C'mon in and have a seat. We're all anxious to meet them."

Moving into the room, Aaron held a hand out toward Kim and Brock. "The little lady is Kim Mackey and the big lug is Brock Odom. Both are damn good agents that I'd trust with my life."

The man stepped over and shook hands with Kim and Brock. "I'm Travis Argent. They tell me I'm in charge of the investigation." Travis laughed. "Serving under the direction of Aaron of course."
Travis turned to the three still seated at the table. "It'll be easier if I let the three of you introduce yourselves."

The other woman in the room was the first to nod and speak. The turquoise colored eyes seemed more intense set off against her jet black hair. "I'm Rachel Moore."
Rachel looked at both agents, but focused her attention n Kim. "The two of us are going to be working together."
Pulling out the chair closest to her, Rachel smiled. "Might as well sit next to me. We'll be spending a lot of time together."

Kim frowned, but knowing she'd be filled in soon about what Rachel had shared, took the seat. She shook hands with the woman after she did. "Nice to meet you. Glad to be working with you."

Across the table, Kim was greeted by two men smiling. The first to speak was a man in his fifties with a bald head and light blue eyes. "I'm Paul West. Nice to meet you Kim."
Paul turned to Brock. "You'll be working with me and this yahoo I call a partner."

Paul pointed at the man next to him who laughed and nodded. He had green eyes, like Brock, but the resemblance stopped easily with the thick red hair the man ran his hand through. "I'm Graham Clark, but everyone calls me Red. I never could figure out why. It's great to meet both of you."

Already deciding he was going to like the new team he was part of, Brock grinned and joined the two men sitting across from Kim and Rachel.
Aaron moved to the far end of the table and took a seat. Travis sat down opposite Aaron. "I want to get the two of you caught up on what's been happening and then I can explain what's next."
Sitting back in his chair, Travis sighed.

"I know Aaron has been giving you updates, so if I repeat anything you already know, you'll just have to let it slide. Of course, both of you know about the seven bombs in the threat. The first six have been located and all were fake. We had a hell of a time trying to get into Treasure Hill resort. The President has convinced a lot of people that the FBI is just trying to frame him. In fact he's asked for yet another investigation into the agency."

The head of brown hair shook wearily.

"I'm sure that news doesn't surprise anyone. It seems he calls for that every other day. Luckily we were able to convince a judge to issue a court order to let us in."

Travis frowned. "We searched the place thoroughly and didn't find even a trace of a bomb."

Shaking her head, Kim frowned. "How can that be? The other places all had the bombs, although inactive, they were set up."

Beside Kim, Rachel nodded. "And that's why we're so worried. The President is going to be here in a couple of days. He's going to speak at that damn grand opening of his. We're worried the bomber is planning on setting off a real bomb during that ceremony."

Leaning forward in his chair, Travis stared at Kim and then over at Brock. "Rachel's right. What she didn't tell you is the resort has actually been up and running for a month or two. There's no reason for the President to even have an opening ceremony. Despite his now knowing about the bomb threats, he insists on the ribbon cutting happening."

Red grunted. "Pompous ass is what I say. All the extra security is always a pain and having the bomb threat makes it worse. Just thank our lucky stars the President's daughter and son-in-law decided to go skiing in Colorado instead of joining him in the ceremony. Those two are almost worse than the president himself."

Shaking his head, Travis pointed a finger at Red. "Keep those opinions to yourself Red. You know we all feel the same, but best for now to let things ride. Sooner or later, the President will get his due. Don't forget, he's under a hell of a lot more investigations that any person or agency."

Travis sighed. "That brings us to the present. We've come up with about the only plan we have available to us. Rachel is working inside the Treasure Hotel. The resort has a buffet, a full service restaurant, a spa, a bar and several shops."

Rachel nodded. "What the restaurant really does is offer a full time buffet along with the restaurant. I'm a hostess and a server." Rachel turned to Kim smiling. The incredible turquoise eyes sparkled with humor as she stared.

"Rick Manor runs the buffet. He was looking for another hostess. Of course, I gave a glowing recommendation for my cousin Kim. That's the story we'll be telling everyone. The boss knows that both of us are with the FBI. You'll like Rick. He said you could start tomorrow."

Kim's own, brown eyes grew large. "Good to know we're cousins. Sounds like you've been busy. I hate to tell you this, but I don't know anything about buffets or any other restaurant work for that matter."

Rachel laughed. "You'll fit right in then."

Travis looked at his watch. "Which reminds me, you're already late for your shift Rachel. You better get out of here. Do you have a spare key to your apartment for Kim?"

Reaching in her pocket, Rachel nodded. Pulling out a key on a small ring, she handed it to Kim. "We're going to be roomies. My apartment only has one bedroom, but I have a couch with a pull-out bed. Make yourself at home. I get off at eleven tonight."

Taking the key, Rachel shook her head, amazed at how inviting all the people on the team were being. "Are you sure? I can always get a motel room."

Rachel smiled. "No need for that. It will be a lot easier to complete this investigation if you're not only staying with me, but also working the same job."
Rachel stood up. "I guess it's off to work for me. It was nice to meet both of you. I'll see you tonight Kim."
With that said, Rachel hurried out of the room. The resort was already short-handed and Rick Manor hadn't been to happy when she told him she would be late.

With the key in her palm, Kim stared down before lifting her head and looking at Travis. "You really know how to make a lady feel welcome."
A frown line creased Kim's forehead. "If Rachel and I are working in the restaurant of the resort, what about carrying our guns? I'm sure the hotel has rules against that."

Travis nodded. "The judge took care of that also. Rick Manor is your boss at the restaurant, but the FBI has been given clearance, reluctantly, I might add, for our stakeout. Rachel and you will be inside, while the rest of us will be stationed outside looking for problems. Periodically, we are doing searches for any bombs. The other sites the bombs were in were set up ahead of time and were also duds. I have a feeling on the ninth we'll find a different scenario."

Aaron nodded. "On top of all that, we have the Daniel Ortiz angle. That guy knows a lot of secrets. With Rueben Adelman linked to him, the President is only a stone's throw away."

Brock smiled. "Which makes the fact that Adelman has walked away an interesting

166

development. Daniel might be willing to exchange a few secrets for a lighter sentence."

Aaron nodded. "And Hal Ostrum is meeting Daniel at six. I think we should get the two of you settled in and then head over to the jail."

Brock frowned. "If Kim is staying with Rachel, where am I going?"

Red smiled. "You're stuck with me. Since Paul is an old, married man and I'm a young buck with no ties, you're headed to my house."

Looking at the green eyes with the glint of humor in them, Brock knew he was going to get along with Red. In fact, he felt at home at this Montana field office much more than he did at the one back in Washington DC. That thought surprised him. He had to admit the old saying was true, you could take the boy out of the country, but you couldn't take the country out of the boy. When he had left Montana for the bright lights of the big city, Brock never thought he'd be back here, let alone enjoying the place.

Aaron was staring at his watch. "I think if we're going to get back to the jail by six, we should take Brock and Kim to their temporary spots, unload their things and the three of us can head back to the station."

Red stood. "You can follow me to my place and then take Kim over to Rachel's."

A few minutes later, Kim and Brock rode with Aaron as they followed Red's non-descript SUV to his impressive house. Once there, the agents only took the time to unload Brock's things before heading, yet again behind Red, to Rachel's apartment. They repeated the quick procedure, said goodbye to Red, then Aaron, Kim and Brock left for the jail.

Chapter 10

A half hour later, the three agents were sitting in the jail's conference room. The jail didn't have a video link, but the audio had been set up so the three could listen in on the conversation between Daniel Ortiz and the lawyer who had been thrown at him. Something the agents felt was strange and Daniel felt was unforgiveable. He didn't know why Rueben Adelman was really to throw him under the bus, when he knew so many secrets, but he knew he was going to find out.

While the three listened, waiting for the conversation to begin, Daniel tried to get comfortable in the miniscule booth he had been placed in. because he was still in the infirmary, the guards had told him that was the standard procedure for talks.

The small room was about the size of a photo booth you could find in a mall. Looking around the room, Daniel felt a burst of claustrophobia hit.

Pushing away the feeling, Daniel stared ahead of him through the glass window at the man he hoped was going to deliver him out of the mess he was in.

Glancing back at Daniel through the glass pane from the other side, the lawyer's eyes only held that position a moment. Hal Ostrum's attention dropped down, then stopped, seemingly fixated on Daniel's left hand where a snake tattoo could be seen, Hal's mind reeled. The lawyer hoped he could accomplish what he'd been asked to do. Hal knew the consequences if he failed would be swift and almost certainly deadly. That thought had Hal nervously wiping his face with one hand before drawing a deep breath and addressing Daniel.

"My name is Hal Ostrum. I'm here as a favor to Mr. Adelman."
Hal shook his head. "I have to be honest with you Daniel. Things don't look good. Despite that, I have arranged for you to see the judge in ten days to give your plea."

The brown eyes flashed anger as Daniel frowned. "Ten days, what the hell? I thought I'd be getting out of here on bail."

Hal shook his head. "I could check on that. But first, I'd have to ask if you are independently wealthy Mr. Ortiz. Murderers aren't usually released on the own recognizance. The bail, if allowed at all, would be extremely high. On top of the murder charge, you paid Cory Baxter to mail bomb threats to the FBI. You then stalked that young man. When you discovered he had been arrested, you waited around the Deer Valley jail for the sole purpose of killing him. That, is premeditated murder."

The anger was evident by the cords standing out on Daniel's reddened neck. The narrowed glare didn't waver as Daniel spoke. "Damn it, what kind of lawyer are you? I don't have any money. I spent every penny Adelman paid me to get my car. What about the man who paid me that money? I would think it was in Adelman's best interest to bail me out. If I'm stuck in here, the chances of me spilling my guts about what I know are freaking high."

When Hal answered, his words were quiet, but spoken with intensity. Staring through the glass, the lawyer slowly shook his head.

He had been expecting the anger and the threat. It was time to do his job.
"Daniel, do you remember the snake?"

Sitting up straighter in his chair, Daniel nodded. "I remember."

Hal grinned. "That's good Daniel, really good. The snake is awake."
Hal waited for the stilted nod that came from the man on the other side of the glass before continuing. "There will be no bail. You're fortunate to even have me here willing to defend you at all. Hell Daniel, most people facing the charges you are would gladly commit suicide. Even in jail, there is always a way. Think about it Daniel. Years on death row just waiting for the day you get that needle stuck in your arm. The lethal injection that will finally end your suffering. Suicide is better than that."
Hal shook his head. "Hell of a future you have Daniel."

Instead of answering, Daniel stared ahead. The blank gaze not focusing nor seeing what was there.

Across from him, Hal once again stared down at the man's tattoo. "Daniel, it looks like that snake is asleep now."

The dark eyes blinked, then Daniel frowned, feeling disoriented.

Placing his hands on the shelf in front of him, running the length of the glass window, Hal pushed himself to a standing position. "Our time is up for today Daniel. I hope you will remember all we talked about. The ball is in your court now."

Without waiting for a response, Hal Ostrum, lawyer for Daniel Ortiz, turned and walked away.

In the booth like room, Daniel closed his eyes, slumping back in his chair. His mind was blank as he waited for a guard to come and take him back to his hospital bed.

In the much bigger conference room, twenty feet away, Aaron, Kim and Brock exchanged astonished glances.

Green eyes wide, Brock shook his head. "What the hell was that all about?"

Running a hand through her short hair and leaving it standing on end, Kim groaned. "I've never heard a lawyer suggest suicide to a client before. I'd call that more than unethical."

Looking from Kim to Aaron, Brock too was mystified. "Why would Hal Ostrum bring up Daniel's tattoo? Something strange is going on."

Aaron stood. "You're right and we better find that lawyer and ask a few questions. I know he was told his conversations with Daniel were being monitored."

Nodding, Brock also stood. "I'll head out and go find him. I think the two of you better go check on Daniel."
Not waiting for a response, Brock headed out of the room.

Getting out her own seat, Kim joined Aaron and headed for the infirmary. The two found Daniel in his bed. Both were surprised to see him sitting up and looking seemingly unaffected by his recent abnormal talk with his lawyer.

Kim moved closer to the bed. "Daniel, are you okay?"

The man stared over at Kim, but she wondered if he was seeing her. His eyes didn't seem to recognize her. Instead they were blank of expression. He nodded, but didn't answer.

Kim turned to Aaron, who shrugged. "I don't think we'll find any answers here. The best thing we can do is just ask the guards to keep an extra close eye on him for trouble."

Before Kim could answer, Brock came rushing over to them. "Ostrum is gone. He must have hightailed it out of here. I didn't see any sign of him or a car leaving."

Aaron shook his head. "Let's go notify the guards and get out of here. We still have an assignment to work on. We need to head back to headquarters and get you each vehicles and then I want you both to go to the places your staying and get some rest. I'll see what information I can get on Hal Ostrum. I have a feeling I'll be paying his office a visit tomorrow."

Although the trio was nervous about what Daniel might do, for the time being they knew his well-being was in the hands of those in the jail. Just because his lawyer had suggested suicide as an answer, none of them had any proof that the suggestions was meant as an order or that Daniel would listen.

Still, as they left the building, none of the agents could shake the feeling of dread.

Aaron drove back to the FBI building and arranged for Kim and Brock to get SUV's and giving them directions, let them leave.

Brock needed to go to Red's house while Kim had to get to Rachel's apartment. Both agents were hoping they would be able to get in a night of rest.

Chapter 11

While Brock drove to Red's house, Kim headed to the apartment she would be sharing with Rachel. On the way, she was delighted to find a fast food restaurant where she picked up a much needed dinner.

Parking the SUV next to the curb, on the street in front of Rachel's house, Kim grabbed her duffle bag and her food, then walked to the door.

Using the key, Rachel had given her, Kim still felt like an intruder as she stepped into the apartment. Reaching over, she found a switch next to the door and was relieved when a light came on revealing the living room. Moving over to the couch, Kim dropped her duffle and sat down. She needed to text her husband, but her grumbling stomach let her know it had first priority. Digging in the bag, Kim placed her food on the coffee table in front of her. She noticed a remote control at the same time. Grabbing it, she turned on the television and flipped through the channels until she found one of the many twenty four hour news stations. If she hadn't been so accustomed to the horrible news that seemed to flood the airwaves day and night lately, she probably wouldn't have been able to hold down the dinner. She was glad she finished most of the meal before her own organization was next to be listed as headline news. Kim threw the papers her meal had been wrapped in along with the few bites she couldn't finish into the bag while she shook her head at the screen. Clips of an earlier press conference showed the President talking about his Treasure Hill Resort. His speech, at first, was all about the FBI's inefficiency and false claims of a bomb that was never found at the resort. The second half of his speech was the man's usual pompous bragging on what an amazing building he had. Kim hated to hear the President announcing he would still be coming to the resort to officiate the official grand opening. The last thing any of them needed was to have the man around. That didn't even take into account the extra security that would have to be in place. Kim had hoped that on the ninth, which was the date set for the ceremony, things might be cancelled.

Kim sighed and flipped off the television. Standing and grabbing the fast food bag, she headed to the kitchen in search of a garbage can. The apartment was small enough, Kim had no problem finding first the kitchen and then the bathroom before returning to the couch.

Before calling Blake, Kim took the time to remove her shoulder holster. Unzipping her duffle bag, Kim laid it on top of her clothes. Feeling more comfortable, Kim sat back on the couch and pulled out her cell phone. Because of everything that had been happening, she knew she was better off just texting her husband, rather than talking to him. Between her doubts about even being an agent, hearing the presidents rhetoric and the strange conversation between Daniel and his lawyer, Kim knew it would be easy to let secrets slip and pour out her frustrations by sharing them with Brock. That was something she had always been careful not to do in the four years she'd been an agent. She wasn't about to start now.

Instead, Kim texted Blake that she was staying with Rachel, a fellow agent, and the assignment was moving along. She added how much she loved him and that she couldn't wait to get home before signing off with, love you forever and adding her name.

Kim laid the phone on the table when she had finished. Just as she sat back on the couch and got comfortable, the phone rang. Kim smiled thinking Blake had decided a text wasn't enough and grabbed the phone. The smile turned to a frown when the caller ID showed the call was coming from Brock instead. Kim sighed, then half laughed, thinking it wasn't Brock's fault she was hoping for the name on the phone to be her husband's. "Hey Brock, what are you doing. Nothing's wrong is it?"

Brock laughed. "Everything is wrong, but nothing new. I just thought I'd call and see if you made it to Rachel's okay."

Kim nodded. "I made it here and had dinner, now I'm just sitting in the quiet apartment. I tried watching TV, but didn't like what I was hearing. How about you? How are things at Red's?"

Brock laughed. "Couldn't be better. It turns out Red is like a billionaire or something. He lives in a freaking mansion. I don't know why he's holding down a job. He said he inherited the place, but I swear I could fit four of my houses in here. I have to say it is refreshing that he's not snobbish about this wealth of his though. He doesn't even have one imported beer in his fridge."

Kim laughed. "That's good to hear. I hope the two you remember we are working and take it easy." Kim grunted. "Speaking of which, what time are we supposed to back at headquarters in the morning?"

Rolling his eyes, even though he knew Kim couldn't see them, Brock smiled. "Aaron said he'd meet us at eight. And don't worry about me, I know my limitations. Red and I are shooting the breeze over a beer or two, then I'm hitting the sack. Just wanted to tell you to have a good night."

Kim smiled. "Same to you Brock. I'll see you in the morning."

Hanging up the phone, Kim felt her spirits lifted after talking to Brock. She smiled thinking how nice he was to have a partner she got along with.

Leaning back on the couch, Kim closed her eyes. She hadn't realized she had nodded off until she heard the sound of the front door opening. A light sleeper, Kim sat upright and leaned forward toward where her gun was resting in her bag. The sound of Rachel's voice had Kim relaxing and sitting back.

"Hi Kim, hope I didn't scare you. The light was on, so I figured you were awake."

Kim laughed. "I thought I was. I guess I must have fallen asleep."

Moving over to sit in the chair across from Kim, Rachel smiled. "Happens to me all the time. Have you had your dinner?"

Kim nodded. "I grabbed some take out on the way here."

Yawning, Rachel stretched. "How about a cup of hot chocolate? While we drink it, I can fill you in on your new job."

When Kim nodded, Rachel stood. "Let's go out in the kitchen. I've always thought that

was the best talking room in a house."
Rachel laughed. "Even if your house is a
tiny, cramped apartment."

Standing and following Rachel, Kim shook
her head. "I think it's cozy and I like it."
Kim was being honest. She loved the way
Rachel had made the apartment feel
comfortable. Looking around the kitchen,
she noticed the cedar cupboards had
engravings on them. Stepping closer, her
brown eyes widened in delight. The corners
of the cupboards had scroll work that had a
rose in the center. She reached up and ran a
finger along the engraved design.
"This work is amazing."

Behind her Rachel laughed. "Thanks, it took
me a month, but I like it too."

Turning, Kim stared at Rachel. "You did
that? If I was that artistic I would be
working anywhere except the FBI."
Kim sighed. "Especially these days."

With a nod, Rachel motioned toward the
table. "Take a seat. I'll get that hot chocolate
started and we can talk."

Kim was surprised when Rachel pulled out a saucepan and ingredients to make the cocoa the old fashioned way. She never seemed to have time anymore for anything culinary. By the time she got home from her job and Blake did the same, the two usually settled for take-out or microwave dinners. Kim shook her head, just another downside to being an agent that she could add to her growing list.

A few minutes later, Rachel slid a mug in front of Kim. Taking her own cup, she sat across the table from Kim. "I know what you mean about being an FBI agent these days. Our jobs are hard enough without the President always degrading our organization and calling for investigations every other day. I don't know how you feel, but to me he's only trying to cover his backside for when the investigations into him are done. He'll twist and turn the facts and find a way to shove the blame onto our agency and others like it. I can only hope the special council closes all loopholes before he presses charges."

Kim shrugged. "I'm just hoping charges are filed. If congress has control, I'm scared nothing will come of all that hard work." Staring at Rachel, Kim leaned forward and frowned. "What about these bombings? Do you think the President is involved? Or do you think his employees finally got fed up and decided to do something about their boss?"

A smirk covered Rachel's face. "One of the first things I was warned about at the resort, was we're not supposed to mention the President owns the place. The bosses there are the President's sons." Rachel laughed. "Although I've never seen them at the place since I've been there and I doubt if the actual employees have either."
The turquoise eyes darkened. "I can't see the President being behind this. His resorts are like children to him. In fact, I think he cares more about the buildings than he does his own kids."

Kim nodded. "He has been known to brag. Even when he doesn't deserve to be. So, if not the President, I'd say it has to be disgruntled workers. I bet he pays them

below minimum and then belittles the immigrant workers he hires."
A sigh escaped as Kim shook her head. "Someone paid Daniel Ortiz a lot of money though. Brock and I were told that car he was driving was worth two or three hundred thousand dollars. He also called Rueben Adelman, who is the white house lawyer."

Rachel shook her head. "But, Adelman threw Daniel aside like an old rag. Daniel probably thought because he worked at Many Lakes he could get help from the President's lawyer. I'm sure as often as the President golfs at that place, Daniel met Adelman at some time or other."

Kim shrugged, "Don't forget, an actual bomb wasn't found at Treasure Hill and the six others that were found were all fakes. I still think this whole thing is a deception. Just another way for the President to make the FBI look bad."

After sipping her cocoa, Rachel set down the mug and smiled. "You could be right, but I don't think we'll get close to figuring out this mystery tonight. Let's talk about something else."

Lifting her cup, in the gesture of a toast, Rachel changed the subject. "How do you feel about starting work at the resort tomorrow afternoon? You'll be working the three to eleven shift with me."

A smile lit up Kim's brown eyes. "Thank goodness we'll be working together." Staring at Rachel, Kim looked at the outfit she was still wearing since coming home from the resort. She liked the black pants and vest, but thought the shiny gold blouse a bit loud. "Is that the outfit you wear for work?"

Rachel nodded. "Yeah, and the company furnishes the clothes."
Seeing the look on Kim's face, Rachel laughed. "The gold is ostentatious isn't it? Even though the President pretends he doesn't own the place, he makes sure there are gold accents everywhere."

Joining in the laughter, Kim nodded.
"I think he feels it makes him look wealthy. Too much of it, does the opposite and looks cheap to me."
A frown replaced the smile. "What about

your gun? There's no room under your blouse and vest for it."

Lifting her leg, Rachel pulled back her pants' leg. "Ankle holster. At work there's also a special entrance for certain workers where you don't have to walk through a metal detector. Rick Manor or one of his assistants checks everyone. Rick makes sure he is on duty during my shifts. He's the only one who knows I'm an FBI agent."
Rachel smiled. "And now that you are."

Kim nodded, impressed. "Sounds to me like you've got things arranged well."
Kim frowned. "Oh wait, what about a Kevlar vest? Anything could happen when the President shows up."

A sly smile played around Rachel's mouth. "I have one stashed in a locked cupboard beneath one of the banquet tables. We can put one there for you too. They might be hard to get to if things get crazy, but we don't have much choice."

Sitting back in her chair, Kim nodded. "I can work with that."

Taking a drink from her cup, Rachel set it down and smiled. "Enough about work and all the craziness of this investigation. Tell me about you. I know you and Brock came from the DC office, but not much else. Are you married? Do you have kids?"

Thinking of Blake, Kim smiled and nodded. "I'm married to about the greatest guy in the world. Blake is a cop and a damn good one. I'm not just saying that because I'm his wife. The guy has a wall full of commendations. He's humble about it though, which makes him even more special. We don't have any children. I wouldn't mind having a couple though. Lately, I've even thought about taking a leave of absence and actually making that idea a reality. What about you?"

Rachel laughed. "Not much to tell, no husband, no kids and right now, I'm not thinking about either. I guess being an agent is my love and my life. I can't imagine doing anything else."
Rachel shook her head, making her black hair swing. "I like to putter around with woodworking, but it isn't something I'd care

to do as my life's work."

Taking the last drink of her coffee, Rachel yawned. "And for tonight, I think I'm talked out. Let me rinse these cups and make the coffee for morning."

Kim started to stand to help, but Rachel shook her head. "Just sit there. I got this." Taking the cups, Rachel looked at Kim. "Do you like morning showers or evenings?"

Surprised by the question, Kim shrugged. "I like morning showers. They help get me started."

Rachel laughed. "Perfect, I like evening showers. In fact, I think I'll grab one and then head to bed. Before I do, I'll show you how to fold out that couch into a bed. I hate to be a party pooper, but my feet are killing me."

Kim smiled. "That's okay, I have to be at headquarters at eight in the morning. What about you? Are you heading in then?"

Standing at the sink, Rachel shook her head and half turned toward Kim while she finished washing the few dishes. "No, with me working at the resort, Travis just has me come in a couple hours before my shift to get briefed. I'll set the coffee to perk at six so you can have some in the morning. I sleep like a log, so don't worry about waking me. You can have your shower then. Just come by the resort about twenty minutes early and I'll get you set up and settled in."

An hour later, Rachel had finished showering and gone to bed.

Kim was in her own bed on the hide-a-bed couch and waiting for sleep to come. After talking to Rachel, Kim found her idea of leaving the FBI was sounding better and better. She couldn't wait for this mission to be over.

Chapter 12

The next morning, despite Rachel telling her not to worry about waking her, Kim was tiptoeing through the quiet house. After her shower and a much needed cup of coffee, Kim folded up the bed and headed out of the apartment. She left her duffle bag, but slipped on her shoulder holster and grabbed her vest before heading for the FBI headquarters.

Pulling into the lot, Kim was surprised to see Brock standing beside an FBI issued SUV. He waved as Kim pulled in, letting her know, her partner had been waiting for her.

Getting out of her own SUV, and seeing the look on Brock's face, Kim knew something was wrong. She stepped over to Brock, a nervous look filling her brown eyes. "What's going on now? Something's wrong isn't it?"

With a sigh, Brock nodded. "Daniel Ortiz is
dead. He took his own life early this
morning. Aaron called me and I told him I'd
talk to you. I didn't see any reason to wake
you up and tell you the news over the phone.
I thought an in person update would be
better."

Although, Daniel's suicide was something
she had worried about since over hearing the
conversation the day before, it was still a
shock. Running both hands through her
short blonde hair, Kim groaned. "Oh hell,
his lawyer really was demanding Daniel
commit suicide."
The brown eyes frowned. "Why wasn't
someone watching him? That doesn't make
any sense."

Shaking his head, Brock shrugged.
"I haven't gotten the whole story yet.
Somehow Daniel got hold of a piece of
metal and slit not only his wrists, but his
own throat."

Leaning over slightly, Kim's arms encircled
her stomach. Fighting the urge to throw up,
Kim finally straightened when Brock placed
a hand on her shoulder. Wiping her

trembling mouth, Kim tried to give Brock a reassuring smile. "I'm okay, I just can't believe this has happened, especially after that strange conversation between Daniel and Hal Ostrum."

Brock nodded. "Aaron and Travis Argent have been trying to reach Ostrum ever since the news of Daniel's death was shared."

Shaking her head, Kim sighed. "I'm guessing Ostrum isn't available for questioning."

Brock gave Kim a sarcastic grin. "You're assumption is right. Let's get inside and see if anything has changed."
When the two began walking toward the building, Brock frowned. "One more thing. I talked to Walt this morning. Cory's funeral is tomorrow at ten. He wanted us to attend, but said he understood if we couldn't."

Sadness could be seen in the brown eyes, followed by conviction. "I'm going to Cory's funeral no matter what comes up. I feel like we owe him at least that."

Brock nodded. "I feel the same. We can head to Deer Valley in the morning. After the funeral we can head back and still leave you plenty of time for working at Treasure Hill resort."

Rolling her eyes, Kim grunted. "Something I'm not looking forward to. I have a feeling people that hang out at the President's properties, aren't the type I like to spend time with. Let's just hope we come up with something so we can close this investigation and go home."

Brock frowned, hearing the despair in Kim's words. "Are you okay? I know this assignment is turning out to be more than we expected, but is there something else bothering you?"

Kim smiled, though her eyes still held sadness. "I'm okay, just ready to get to the bottom of things."

Brock nodded. "Me too, let's go inside and see if anyone has come up with anything."

The two headed into the FBI building and headed to the room where they had met their colleagues the day before. When they entered, only Aaron was in the room. He looked at his agents when they entered. It wasn't hard to tell Brock had shared the news of Daniel Ortiz's suicide. He focused his attention on Kim. "I'm sorry you had to start your day with the horrific news. From what I was told, the jail had a guard on Ortiz. That guard had to be put in the hospital. I was told Daniel was crazy and determined to kill himself. He attacked the guard before grabbing a knife and slicing his wrists and then his own throat. I'm sure now Daniel Ortiz was somehow under hypnosis and had been given directives, maybe even years ago, to commit suicide. I think Hal Ostrum was the man given the task to deliver those instructions. His job done, it looks like Mr. Ostrum has vanished. We have an all-points bulletin out for his arrest." Aaron motioned at the chairs by the conference room table. "Both of you can take a seat and I'll fill you in on our agenda. Travis, Paul and Red headed over to the resort about an hour ago."

When Kim and Brock found chairs, Aaron joined them at the table. It took a couple of hours for Aaron to fill the two in on what their jobs would be. Kim and Rachel would be inside the resort, while the rest of the agents would take up positions on the outside. They expected the President, along with his secret service agents to show up early in the evening the night on the eighth.

When Kim heard that, she frowned. "I thought the opening ceremony was on the ninth. Why is the President coming early? He could show up on the morning of the ninth and still have time for that ceremony."

Aaron grunted. "He's coming the night of the eighth so he can be noticed would be my guess. The ceremony is still set for the ninth. That is also the day the last bomb is set to go off. Right now, all I can say is keep your eyes and ears open. I should tell you, although the President's daughter and son-in-law declined to attend, his sons are already at the resort."

Kim moaned. "Looks like this is my day for hearing bad news. Hopefully the two of them will be anywhere but the buffet I'm assigned to work."
Kim frowned. "Which reminds me. Rachel has worked it out so we can carry our guns and hide some vests if we need them, but what if I need to contact you or Brock?"

Aaron shook his head. "You're going to have to use your cell phone. The resort has its' own communications system you'll be using and that would interfere with our system. I'm sorry about that, I'd rather have a live and direct line from you to us."

With a shrug Kim smiled. "That's alright, I have both Brock and you on speed dial."

Aaron looked at his watch. "It's time for me to head to the resort. Why don't the two of you take time out for a lunch break and then head over?"

Just over an hour later, Kim and Brock had finished lunch and made their way to the resort. Brock joined the other agents outside while Kim headed to the door Rachel had told her about. The place where she could be let into the building without having her gun set off an alarm.

Rachel was waiting with Rick Manor to let Kim enter. Rachel smiled. "Glad you're early. Let's go find you some clothes. Oh, by the way, this is Rick. He's been good enough to work with us. He's the only person in the resort that knows who we actually are."

Kim exchanged greetings with Rick and then followed Rachel down a hall with golden wallpaper. Rachel lifted a hand and motioned toward the distasteful wall covering. "Does the whole resort look like this?"

Rachel laughed. "This looks good compared to the rest of the resort. The President thinks it looks luxurious. Maybe if we see him, we can tell him the opposite is true."

Kim shook her head. "Personally, I'd rather not make his acquaintance."

Entering a fairly large dressing room, Kim was given black pants with a matching vest. She frowned when Rachel handed her the gold shirt she was also required to wear. Kim took it and shook her head. "Let's hope this assignment is wrapped up quickly."

After Kim changed, Rachel showed her to the buffet room. The place was enormous, with a rounded ceiling towering thirty feet above the area. Kim's brown eyes widened.

"I hate to admit it and even with the cheap gold touches, this place is incredible."

Rachel shook her head. "This is nothing. Wait until you see the dining room, bar and conference rooms. I think the place has at least ten different specialty rooms."

Kim sighed. "I'll probably get lost."

Rachel laughed. "I'll make sure and keep an eye on you then. Right now, let me show you how the buffet system here works."

Two hours later, Kim was getting used to the routine. Mostly she greeted people and made sure all the food containers were full. As soon as they were close to empty, Kim had to use her communication device to call the kitchen and then run to the place for a replacement container filled to the brim with a variety of foods. Putting the bins in place, Kim realized there were several with concoctions she didn't recognize.

Halfway through her shift. Kim was surprised when Rachel walked toward her carrying a round, flat tray with several drinks on it. "I think you should be the one to deliver these drinks to the dining room. If you take them to the table in the far right corner of the room, you'll find the President's sons bragging loudly to a friend they have with them."

The brown eyes widened as Kim nodded, hoping this was a chance to overhear something that might help solve the mystery they had on their hands. Adjusting the headset she wore to communicate with the rest of the staff, Kim took the tray and smiled. "Wish me luck."

Rachel nodded and watched Kim walk away carefully as she tried to balance the drink tray.

Stepping into the dining area for the first time, Kim stopped abruptly and stared around her. The place was triple the size of the buffet room. Even though the lighting was low, Kim could easily see the elegantly dressed diners. She looked over to the far right side of the room and began walking.

Weaving a path through the tables wasn't as hard as she had worried it might be. Apparently guests at the President's resort liked their elbow room. Kim was grateful for that. She had never been a waitress and was afraid the drinks she so carefully carried would topple over at any moment. She heard the sound of loud laughter well before she reached the table where the President's sons sat with another man about the same age as the two. The way all three were sitting and talking, Kim felt the arrogance that hung around their table was like the smoke that lingered in a lounge in an old black and white movie.

Moving to the table, Kim felt invisible when no one even turned to look at her. Removing the drinks from the tray, she congratulated herself on a job well done. The three at the table didn't bother with thanks. They only grabbed their drinks and continued talking.

Moving from the table to one empty of guests, but still covered with dishes a few feet away, Rachel was glad for the insignificance placed on her. Although it was a disgrace for people to treat others in such a derogatory manner, for Rachel it was a stroke of luck. It gave her the chance to listen in on the conversation.

Kim was amazed by the thread of the conversation and that the President's sons didn't worry about the things they were loudly discussing in a public place. Slowly clearing the table and loading a few things onto the platter she held, Kim listened as the President's sons talked, boasting to their friend.

"By the time our dad is finished no one will trust the FBI or any intelligence agency in America. The special council's word won't be worth a plug nickel. Having Daniel Ortiz shut up for good, seals that deal."

The friend who had been listening raptly, shook his head. "You've got it all figured out. The best part is while everyone is chasing stories, your family is making millions. I really appreciate your dad getting me those government contracts. Walcott Construction just began trading on the stock exchange. Can you believe it?"
The man frowned. "What about your sister? I heard that she and that husband of hers were causing some trouble."

Both brothers started laughing, but again it was the older, dark haired brother who spoke. "Don't worry about the little princess or her husband. Dad's got plans for them. The two were only invited along for the ride hoping they would sway liberal votes. Her husband, the phony prince, is in debt up to his eyeballs. Even if dad doesn't fire him, he is facing criminal charges for his double dealings. We need to distance ourselves or get caught up in the whole sordid thing. I'd rather the country's money we're raking in go to old, loyal friends like you."

The man smiled and nodded. "Well, like I said, I appreciate that."

The brothers both laughed and raised their glasses in a toast. The darker haired brother grinned. "What are friends for?"

The sound of a voice coming through her ear piece startled Kim and she jumped. One of the dishes fell with a crash onto the floor. Kim's gaze immediately went to the table where the three men sat. Unfortunately they were also staring at her, looks of distaste on their faces. Kim leaned down and grabbed the plate, while trying to hear the person speaking to her on the communication device.

"Kim, where are you? You're supposed to be helping at the buffet."

Flustered, Kim stacked the dishes again while she answered. "Sorry about that. I'm on my way."

Ignoring the looks she was getting, Kim grabbed the tray and hurried as fast as she could without creating another accident and headed out of the dining room to the buffet area.

Stepping into the buffet area, Kim was met by a harried looking young man whose name she couldn't remember.

"About time you got here. Where were you?"

Holding the tray full of dirty dishes awkwardly, Kim sighed. "Rachel asked me to help out in the dining room."

The young man shook his head, rolling his eyes to complete the motion. "Take those dishes into the kitchen. I've already called back and told them what we need refills on out here. You can grab the supplies on your way back. Then you can take over as hostess for a while. My break is already twenty minutes overdue."

Wanting to tell the guy where he could shove his break, Kim swallowed the retort and headed for the kitchen. On the way, she took the time to call Rachel on the headset. "Rachel, I need to get hold of Brock but I can't get away from the buffet."

In the bar, Rachel carried drinks to a table and set them down before answering. She was certain, by the sound of Kim's voice, her fellow agent had heard something in the dining room. Exactly what Rachel had hoped for when she'd sent Kim there. "Give me a few minutes to finish up in here and then I'll come and cover for you."

Grateful for the help. Kim blew out her pent up frustration and tried to calm down. "Thanks a lot Rachel."

Making her way into the kitchen, which was bigger than any Kim had seen before, she got rid of the dirty dishes. Kim then grabbed the several containers of food someone had set up and returned to the buffet. She gladly told the young man to take his break as she began replenishing the buffet. She spoke to the guests who were filling their plates and tried to be helpful. Even with all that, time seemed to stand still. Rachel's mind unfortunately was doing the opposite. The conversation she'd been advantageous enough to eavesdrop on, floated round and round in her thoughts.

By the time Rachel stepped in the room, Kim felt like her head was going to explode.

Stepping up to her, Rachel could see the anxiety. "Go on and make your call. When we get home tonight though, I want to hear every sorted detail."

Kim managed a relieved smile and a thanks before heading in search a secluded spot to call Brock. She ended up in one of the resorts many restrooms. She waited impatiently for a middle aged woman to quit primping in front of a mirror and leave before she finally pulled out her phone and paced the call.

Outside the building, Brock stood with Red. The two agents were fifty feet away from the main entrance to the resort. Both kept close watch on the crowd going in and coming out of the building. Although a long line of patrons waited, showing irritation with the extra security, Brock knew that was only going to get worse. People knew the President was coming. It would seem many wanted their chance at whatever piece of pie the man was doling out. Brock also noticed many of the people had arrived in chauffer driven limousines. By the clothes some were wearing, Brock had come to the conclusion those people weren't from America either. He knew the President was known to hob knob with world leaders that weren't known to be this country's allies.

Scanning the faces, Brock felt the vibration of his cell phone in his back pocket where he'd tucked it in earlier. Grabbing the phone, Brock stared at the caller ID before turning to Red. "It's Kim."

Brock turned slightly away from Red and the crowd, but still kept one eye on the events going on around him as he answered. "Kim, what's going on? Is everything okay?"

In the bathroom, Kim stood where she could keep watch on the door. She didn't want anyone listening in on the conversation she wanted to share. "I'm not sure. The President's sons are in the dining room with a friend. I was able to get close enough to listen in on their conversation."

Kim grunted. "Actually, they were talking loud enough anyone who wanted to, could hear. The gist of their boasting was about the President and confirms what we felt all along. The President's agenda is to discredit all intelligence agencies and make it so no one will believe any charges the special council comes up with. One of the rumors I heard about is true though. I listened to the President's sons say their own sister and her husband were headed out of the white house. The two of them seemed happy instead of upset about that prospect. They knew about Daniel Ortiz too, saying they were glad he was out of the way. The friend who was with them was falling all over himself giving thanks to the President. It seems this guy is making a lot of money thanks to some lucrative government contracts."

Brock frowned trying to follow Kim's rambling explanation, but the last thing she said caught his radar. "Who is this guy? He's definitely someone I'd be interested in talking to, maybe someone we could get some dirt on and flip to our side.”

Kim also had a frown on her face. “I didn’t hear his name, but the company is called Walcott Construction.”

The sound of Brock’s disgusted groan could be heard before he answered. “Oh hell, the guy is Jefferson Walcott. In the last six months, his two bit construction company is suddenly in high demand. Mr. Walcott and his company are also the subject of at least a half a dozen lawsuits. Their subpar work, failure to meet deadlines and tendency to go well over budget raised a lot of red flags. It’s been on the news. I’m surprised you haven’t seen it.”

Rachel laughed. “So much is happening in the news every day, I can’t catch everything.”

Glad to hear Rachel laughing, Brock smiled. “You’re forgiven. I’ll get the word out to watch for Walcott. Maybe we’ll get lucky and find a way to grab him.”
Brock drew in a breath. “Oh damn, that reminds me. Our friend and not so favorite

lawyer Hal Ostrum was picked up. Aaron and Travis headed back to headquarters to meet with him. The police are taking him their instead of jail for the time being. If we can get some info from him, Ostrum might get out of the jail time."

Kim sighed. "The guy deserves jail time after what he did. Ortiz's death is on Ostrum's head."

Brock nodded. "It is, but someone put Ostrum up to it. Probably Reuben Adelman, but remember they all take orders from our President."

Kim didn't want to even think about that. She knew the President was committing illegal activities but she didn't want to think ordering a murder was part of that agenda. "Hopefully they can get Ostrum to spill what he knows in order to save his hide."

Brock shrugged. "You never know. Is everything else going okay?"

Kim smiled. "It is unless I don't get back out and do my job."

Brock laughed. "Back to feeding the snobs for you then. Thanks for filling me in. If anything else strange happens I want to hear about it. Don't forget, we're going to Deer Valley in the morning. I'll pick you up at eight and buy you breakfast."

Kim nodded. "I'll be ready although I may not have an appetite."

Brock grinned. "I can eat anytime. I'll finish what you don't want."

Kim laughed. "It's a deal, see you in the morning."

Hanging up the phone, Kim stepped to the door and opened it just as someone was pushing it inward from the other side. Glad the timing hadn't been a few minutes earlier, Kim headed back to the buffet to take her job back from Rachel.

Chapter 13

Kim was up and waiting for Brock long before he arrived. Despite the fact that she had sat up late and explained what she had heard from the President's sons to Rachel. After that, the two had discussed the possibilities of the President being behind not only Ortiz's death, but the bomb threats for another hour before both, yawning and with red eyes, finally went to bed.

Kim's earlier idea to skip her morning coffee until Brock arrived and took her to a restaurant changed as the smell of fresh brewed coffee filled the apartment.

Heading to the kitchen, Kim filled a mug, then carried it to the living room. Standing at the window, she pulled back the curtain so she could watch for Brock.
Kim dreaded the thought of going to Cory's funeral. She was also aware of the fact that nothing would prevent her from attending. Guilt over Cory Baxter's death was

something Kim knew she'd carry with her the rest of her life.

When Brock hadn't shown up by the time her cup was empty, Kim hurried to the kitchen and washed her mug. Returning to the front room, Kim resumed her watch. Brock pulled in a few minutes later.
Kim hurried out the front door, locking the sleeping Rachael in the apartment. The two had already made plans to meet at the resort a few minutes before their three o'clock shift. Kim only hoped the investigation would break and she wouldn't have to endure any more shifts.

Getting in the SUV, Kim gave Brock a half-grin. The way she was feeling that was all she could muster.

Brock smiled back before reaching over and touching Kim's shoulder. "I know how you feel about Cory's death. I agree we are partially responsible, but Daniel Ortiz would have killed Cory whether we were there or not. The least we can do to honor Cory's memory is to close this case. Ortiz was as much a victim as Cory."

Frowning, Kim nodded. "Yeah and you know who is behind all of this. How are we supposed to take down the President of the United States? Look at all the illegal and immoral things the guy has done already. Nothing seems to stick to that man."

Brock nodded. "I know how you feel, but people are dying. We'll make this stick Kim. I won't stop until we do."
Brock started the car. "Let's go get some breakfast. Thinking about that man is hard to do on an empty stomach."

Kim nodded although she hated the thoughts of the man and what he was doing whether her stomach was empty or full.

It only took a few minutes to reach the restaurant, then head in and find a booth that sat in a secluded corner. After the waitress took the pair's order, she left them alone with full cups of coffee sitting in front of them.

Taking a drink of his coffee, Brock placed the cup on the table, then leaned toward Kim. His green eyes lit up. "I do have some good news. I was so worried about how you were feeling about the funeral today it slipped my mind."

Kim sighed. "If you have some good news, I'd love to hear it. I could use a pick-me-up."

Brock nodded. "First, Ostrum is talking. So far, Aaron has only hit the tip of the iceberg. I have a feeling Hal Ostrum doesn't think he'd fare well in jail. That guy is out to save his own skin. Second, and I hope even better, we arrested Jefferson Walcott when he left Treasure Hill last night. Not only does Mr. Walcott have a lead foot when he's been drinking, but he enjoys smoking pot. The cops found marijuana in his car along with an assortment of paraphernalia when they stopped him for speeding. Of course, his mandatory call was to his lawyer, but I think Jefferson may have a few secrets about the President's family. Not only is Walcott also a man who wouldn't do well in jail, but he won't want bad publicity now that his business is raking in the dough."

Now, Kim was the one leaning forward. A grin covered her face as she felt her hopes

rise. Maybe this case would be over soon after all. The brown eyes that had lit up suddenly darkened as a frown replaced the smile. "Damn it Brock. Why'd you take so long to share that information?"
She shook her head and smiled. "Never mind. I'm just happy to hear it."

The two discussed the case, keeping their voices quiet, until the waitress brought their food. After the good news, Kim found she had an appetite again and gladly dug into her breakfast.

By the time the meal was finished and the two were back in the SUV headed to Deer Valley, Kim wished she hadn't eaten. Anxiety about attending the funeral was making her queasy.

Brock drove straight to the funeral home. Entering the building, Kim and Brock were given a hearty reception by Walt. Both were a little surprised not to see any of Cory's family doing the greeting. Instead, Walt stood alone in the funeral home vestibule. He pointed at a guest book sitting on a small table. "I'd love both of you to sign the book and then you can go on in and find a seat.

We still have a few minutes before the actual funeral starts."

Although Walt had greeted both Brock and herself with a hug when they had entered, Kim gave him another before following Brock's example and signing the book. The two left Walt and went in finding a seat a few rows back from where a coffin took center stage. The room wasn't packed, but dozens of people already sat talking quietly while waiting for the funeral to start. The agents were both surprised not to see a sectioned off place for family.

A preacher walked in followed by Walt. The two men took seats by the podium sitting behind Cory's casket. The preacher stood up first and after greeting the crowd, read a short obituary that covered Cory's life. Finished with that, the preacher sat and Walt stood. Nervously adjusting the microphone to his over six foot height, Walt cleared his throat a few times before he began talking.

"Most of you know me. For those who don't I am the sheriff here in Deer Valley. I was with Cory Baxter when he was murdered. Cory was a good kid who made some bad mistakes. Trying to better himself, Cory made a deal for money. A bargain that got him killed. I wasn't with Cory just because of my job as sheriff. I felt like Cory was family. Anyone from Deer Valley could tell you that Cory's mom was also like family to me. In fact, I loved Evie. After she died, I felt responsible for Cory. His dad, Lance Baxter, had his own problems and wasn't the father figure Cory needed. Sadly, I failed Evie and Cory. I only hope the two of them are together in Heaven and they will forgive me."

Kim, watching Walt struggle with his own emotions, felt tears sting her eyes. Beside her, Brock felt the same. He had always felt Walt and Cory had a special relationship. Although he didn't know the whole story, Brock was sure that Walt would have gladly taken Lance Baxter's place as Cory's dad. Sadly love and relationships don't always turn out with happy endings. His heart ached for what Walt was going through.

In front of the crowd, Walt wiped his eyes. "None of us knows what decisions we make will end wrong. I only hope you will

remember Cory Baxter as the loving young man he was. He was a hard worker and rose above life's challenges. I will never stop missing him."
Walt cleared his throat again. "If anyone else would like to stand and share a memory, you are welcome to do so."

A few people in the audience stood and told stories about Cory. His boss echoed Walt's words about Cory's work ethics, while a couple of Cory's friends stood and told their own tales. Listening to them, Kim wondered why, even though Cory's parents were dead, no grandparents or other relatives were making their presence known. Kim sighed knowing that was a mystery she didn't have the time to find out. Brock and her had enough on their plates with the investigation.

After the few people spoke, the preacher once again stood to give a prayer and ask all to head to the graveyard for the burial.

At the cemetery, the preacher once again offered a prayer as Cory Baxter's body was laid to rest.

Kim and Brock headed over to Walt. After refusing the offer to stay in town for a luncheon that was being given by the women of the church, Brock decided to fill Walt in on some the news concerning Cory's killer. "Daniel Ortiz committed suicide. I'm sure you heard about that. I want you to know that we have a few leads on this investigation and hope to find the people responsible for sending Ortiz to kill Cory. Kim and I both want you to know we aren't going to let those responsible get away with this."

Nodding, Walt sighed. "I never doubted that. I want to thank both of you for showing up today. It meant a lot to me. I'm sure Cory was glad you were here too. I know you both need to get back to Helena and I have my own responsibilities. Thanks again for coming. I'd love to hear what happens if you can tell me after your investigation is over."

Brock and Kim both nodded before telling Walt good-bye. The two left the cemetery and headed for the FBI office in Helena.

As Brock drove, he noticed Kim was quiet, but was at a lost for any words that were adequate given the situation.

When they pulled in at FBI headquarters, both got out of the car. Kim frowned at Brock. "You go on in. I'll be up in a minute. I just wanted to text my husband and tell him things might be improving. Blake doesn't know any specifics about the investigation, but he knows I've been frustrated."

Brock smiled. "I'll meet you upstairs then."

Waiting until Brock went in the door, Kim then pulled out her phone. Knowing Blake was at work, although she wanted to hear his voice, Kim decided on sending a text.

"We have a couple of leads on the case. Hoping to be done with this mess and home soon. I miss you so much. Love you forever."

After she finished sending the text, Kim slipped her phone in her pocket. She had only taken a couple steps toward the building when she heard the familiar dinging sound meaning she had a text coming in.

Pulling her phone back out, Kim smiled as she read the message.

"I miss you more. Hurry home, the boss says my vacation starts the minute you get here. Forever is a long time, but never long enough because I love you more than anything in the world."

Slipping her phone back in her pocket, Kim felt like she was gliding on air as she made her way to the conference room.
Stepping in, Kim was surprised to see an unfamiliar face sitting at the table with Aaron, Travis and Brock.

Seeing Kim, Aaron stood. "Glad you're here Kim. I don't think you've actually met Hal Ostrum. He's here to cooperate with our team."

Staring at the man whose voice she had heard, but whose face she hadn't seen, Kim was surprised. In her mind, she had put a face to the voice, but of course, the pictures didn't match up to reality. The man looking up at her looked to be in his fifties, older than she had imagined. The blue eyes were light colored and looked compassionate.

Kim had been expecting cruel eyes with no light to them. She nodded at the man in greeting before taking her seat.

Aaron sat beside her. "Mr. Ostrum was just explaining to us that this was the only time he has been asked to help Rueben Adelman, the Presidents legal council."

Hal Ostrum nodded. His head of thinning brown hair bouncing up and down enthusiastically. "That's right. Rueben is a longtime friend, but we don't mix work with pleasure. This is the first time he asked me a favor."

Hal shook his head. "I shouldn't have gotten involved and I'm really sorry that Daniel Ortiz ended up taking his own life. When Rueben told me that might happen, I didn't actually believe it. Sadly, when Rueben said he had used suggestive hypnosis many times before, I still thought it was some kind of joke. Even before Rueben worked in the White House, he was friends with the man who would end up as President, for years. The two of them used the same treatment on business associates to make money."

The brown eyes widened as Kim stared at Hal. "Are you telling us the President is really behind this? Behind Daniel Ortiz's death and even Cory Baxter's?"

The man nodded. "I'm telling you the truth. And not just to save my own skin either. What these people are doing is immoral. I only wished I would have talked to the law years ago. With the power behind the Presidency backing these people, anything could happen. I swear, I didn't know anything about Daniel Ortiz when I got the call from Rueben. When I talked to Daniel and told him that many people in his situation committed suicide, I honestly didn't think he would try it."

Aaron frowned. "Did you know Daniel Ortiz was ordered to kill Cory Baxter?"

Hal shook his head. "No, I knew Daniel was in jail for murder, but didn't know anything about the events that got Daniel arrested. To tell you the truth, I haven't been in communication with Rueben for a couple years. I wish I wouldn't have answered his call this time. Believe me, no one wants to stop these people as much as I do. I hate myself for causing Daniel Ortiz's death. The only way I know how to compensate for my part in that is to try and help you to stop them before more damage and deaths occur."

Seeing how upset Hal Ostrum was, Aaron nodded. "I think we could all use a break." Aaron turned to Travis. "Why don't you take Mr. Ostrum and get him a cup of coffee."

Standing, Travis nodded and took hold of Hals' arm. "We'll be back within a half an hour. C'mon Hal, let's go get that drink."

Aaron waited for agent Argent to leave with Hal before turning to Kim and Brock. "I need both of you over to the Treasure Hill resort. Kim, you keep an eye on things inside and Brock you join the others outside. Travis and I are going to get a judge to listen to Hal's story. We are also arranging to talk with Jefferson Walcott. I think he can back up what Hal is saying. as impossible as it sounds. By tonight, tomorrow at the latest, I think we will be able to get an arrest warrant for the President of the United States issued."

Aaron smiled. "And more for all those working with him."

Kim shook her head. "I just can't believe it. I knew the President was up to no good, but I never thought that included hiring murders done."
Kim frowned. "What if he slips out of this like he has everything else?"

Brock shook his head. "Not this time. It looks like the President has finally asked a person with a conscience to do something atrocious. I've been wondering when a person like that would surface. All those yes men he surrounds himself with. Even those I thought had morals and decency were letting him get away with unethical things. I just wish Hal Ostrum would have found that conscience before Cory and Daniel had to die."

Aaron nodded. "Hopefully we can stop the atrocities before another death happens. Hal Ostrum didn't know about the bomb threats, but they had to have been ordered by the President also. Thank God, they were fakes."

Brock looked at his watch. "Kim and I better get to the resort and keep an eye on things. The President's big ceremony is the day after tomorrow. Let's hope no more chaos happens before you get the warrant and we stop him."

Aaron nodded. "We still haven't found the bomb that was supposed to be planted at the resort. Let's just hope our finding the others stopped the plan and that last bomb never shows up."

Kim sighed. "Even if it is fake like the others."
She stood up. "C'mon Brock. Let's go. Maybe this will be one of the last times I have to wear that cheap looking gold shirt."

Brock drove Kim to Rachel's apartment to get her SUV and then followed her to the resort.

Brock parked next to Kim when they pulled in. He headed out to the front of the resort to meet with the other agents, while Kim headed in through the back door in search of Rachel.

Once inside, Kim was relieved to find
Rachel in the dressing room and alone.

Looking at Kim as she entered, Rachel knew
Travis and Aaron had shared the news
concerning Hal Ostrum's willingness to talk.
Travis had called Rachel earlier in the day.
The news had been amazing, but Rachel had
learned through her years as an agent to be
wary. She'd had informants turn on her on
more than one occasion. Rachel smiled at
Kim. "Judging by your face, you've talked
to Travis and Aaron. Looks like things are
falling into place. I swear, you look ten
years younger than you did last night. Did
you meet Hal Ostrum?"

Kim nodded. "I did and even got to hear part
of his story. I don't know how sincere he is
in his regrets about what he did, but I am
thrilled that he is willing to talk, even if it is
just to save his own skin."

Shrugging, Rachel nodded. "Whatever
works. I haven't got the chance to see him
yet. Travis called and updated me in on the
new turn of events. Let's just hope word
doesn't get out that Ostrum is talking."

Kim nodded. "I never thought I'd say it. But I'm thankful the President's sons are already here for the ceremony. At least we have extra help with security."

Nodding, Rachel frowned. "Do you think it's strange his daughter and her husband would rather be skiing?"

Kim shrugged. "Not really. From what I overheard the other night it is easy to see there is no love lost between the brothers and their sister. I get the feeling she was the President's favorite. That could easily be what caused the friction. Jealousy between siblings has caused many altercations. To tell you the truth, I'm glad she's not here. Extra security for the sons is okay, but more family would also mean larger crowds. I think we're already looking at total chaos when the President gets here."

Rachel nodded. "You're right, it's already bad now. All these people wanting their chance to see the son's and get the chance at a backdoor deal with our crooked President."

Kim sighed. "That's an understatement."
Looking at her watch, Kim rolled her eyes.
"Time to dawn the chintzy gold shirts. Why
does the President think the color gold
somehow makes people think he's rich? If
you have to put on a show, you're just as
fake as the fool's gold."

Rachel laughed. "Hang in there Kim. You
may only have to dress like that another
night or two. The President will be here day
after tomorrow."

Kim smiled. "And hopefully we will have an
arrest warrant from the judge to greet him
with."

Holding up her own gold shirt with a look of
distaste, Rachel nodded. "You can say that
again. We don't need this disturbance and
destruction the President is causing. We
have enough to worry about. I can think of
at least two countries who are threatening us
with a nuclear attack. That should be where
are resources are focused. The President
won't even give our agencies the word to
proceed with anything to prevent cyber-
attacks let alone nuclear ones."

Seeing Kim's own disgusted look at her gold shirt, Rachel laughed. "Just put it on quickly, it won't hurt so much. We have work to do. Would you like to try working the bar instead of the buffet tonight?"

Kim shook her head. "I better stick with the buffet. I almost know what I am doing there."

The two walked out of the dressing room and headed their separate ways to start their shifts.

The night went quickly for Kim, with no big problems. By the time her shift ended though, she was looking forward to heading to Rachel's apartment for much needed rest. Even with all her FBI job entailed, she couldn't remember her feet and back hurting so badly.

Chapter 14

The sound of her phone ringing, brought Kim out of the land of dreams. A place she didn't want to leave. Reaching over, she grabbed the phone without looking at the caller ID. "Leave me alone, I'm dreaming."

Holding his phone, Brock wished he was doing anything but calling Kim with more bad news. That seemed to be all he did lately. "Kim, it's ten o'clock. Time to get up. Sadly, I don't think you'll like the reason I'm calling."

Astounded she had slept in so late, Kim sighed. "It's alright. Just spit it out. Do it before I'm fully awake. Maybe I'll take it better that way."

Taking a breath, Brock exhaled loudly before sharing his news. "The President is headed to the resort. He'll be here in a few hours. The plane is already in the air."

Shaking away the last remnants of sleep, Kim's brown eyes grew large. "Oh hell. Things are crazy enough without him showing up even earlier than expected." Kim sat up on the hide a bed. "Do we need to head to headquarters?"

Brock nodded. "We do, but we have time for breakfast before we go in."

Running a hand through her short hair, Kim sighed. "Give me an hour to get ready and we can have lunch instead."

A smile covered Brock's face. Kim was taking this better than he had expected. "Meet me at the diner from yesterday. You'll need your car. After we meet at headquarters it will be time for you to head to work."

Rolling her eyes, Kim sighed. "Don't remind me. I'll see you in an hour."

After saying goodbye, Kim headed in to share the news with Rachel before she rushed in to take a shower and dress.

Just under an hour later she drove to the restaurant. Brock was waiting inside. He waved to her when she entered from a booth not far from the last one they had sat in. Kim hurried over and sat down. "Thanks for calling. Even if it was with terrible news, I slept too long. I must have been more tired out than I thought. Have you ordered yet?"

Brock shook his head and held up a glass filled with a dark liquid. "Just my drink. I told the waitress you'd be here soon."

Kim nodded. "I'm not that hungry, but I better eat something or I'll never make it through what I am sure will be a long shift."

An hour later, the two were headed in separate vehicles to the FBI headquarters. They walked together up to the conference room where not only Aaron and Travis waited, but the other agents as well. Even Rachel had come in for the special meeting before her work at the resort began.

After the two were seated, Travis stood. "Before we even talk about the President's early arrival, I want to give you some good news. We have a judge lined up. He's going to be listening to Ostrum later today. Jefferson Walcott's lawyer is also willing to make a deal and talk to the judge. I'm optimistic we'll be handed an arrest warrant by tomorrow morning at the latest."

Around the room the sound of sighs and a couple of louder positive exclamations could be heard. Kim though, was frowning. "The ceremony is tomorrow. Will you arrest the President then?"

Travis shook his head. "I think that would start a riot. You know how the die-hard followers are. When we get the warrant we'll wait until after the speech. Once the President talks, I think most of those gathered will be heading for the bar. That's when we'll deliver the message and warrant."

Next to Travis, Aaron frowned. "If this ceremony ends up like the President's other rallies, the crowds get damn rambunctious. Let's hope we have plenty of security around. I can understand why the President's daughter and son-in-law would rather be somewhere else. Although, I have to wonder why they always seem to be somewhere when big news breaks, especially when it is not in favor of the

President."

Aaron didn't add to his statement, even though he was looking into that angle and the relationship between the President and the two aforementioned people. Something didn't sit right with that connection to Aaron. He was doing a private search and until he had concrete information he didn't want to share his theories.

At the far end of the table, Kim was nodding. "I've wondered about that myself. The two sons don't seem to care for the daughter or her husband."

Brock smiled. "No matter the reasoning behind the bond or lack of, we have enough on our plates right now in connection with Treasure Hill Resort. I think it's time we head over there."

Looking at his watch, Travis nodded. "Brock's right. the President's plane, if it hasn't already landed, is damn close. Everyone should head out. I'm staying behind to tie up loose ends and hopefully get that warrant signed, sealed and ready for delivery tomorrow. Everyone remember to keep everything we know quiet. Any leaks right now would destroy all we've worked to accomplish."

The rest of the group nodded their understanding and agreement before standing and leaving the room.

Brock and Red walked to the parking lot with Kim and Rachel. Looking at Kim, Brock sighed. "It feels like the two of us have spent more time apart than together on this assignment. I just wanted to tell you, no matter what happens over the next couple of days, I'll feel damn lucky Aaron put us together as partners."

Kim smiled, then stepped over to give Brock a hug. "I feel the same as you do. I just hope all we've been through ends up with the President behind bars. The man has done so much damage in such a short time. I only hope we can get back to the normal we had before the guy was elected. No more lies, no more porn stars, and no more taking people into a downward spiral."

Nodding, Brock gave Kim a big smile that had his green eyes dancing. "We're going to do this. I told you before, I am not giving up and letting this upheaval happen to America and also hurt the rest of the world."

Kim laughed. "Thanks Brock, I feel a lot better. Well, other than now we have to head to the resort."

Stepping over to Kim, both Red and Rachel were shaking their heads. Red shrugged. "At least this is all coming to a head. Whatever happens tomorrow, the world is going to know what the President has been doing."

Rachel sighed. "Hopefully, people will believe the truth this time. The President has discredited all intelligence agencies long enough. It's time to put an end to that and like Kim said, return to some kind of normalcy."

The four agents got in their own vehicles and drove in a small procession to the resort. Once there, Kim and Rachel headed inside while Brock and Red headed to the front of the resort to take their places and try and maintain damage control.

An hour later, Rachel had headed to the bar, while Kim was at the buffet. She was surprised to look up and see the President step into the room. None of his family was with him, but his bodyguards had spread out watching carefully for trouble while trying not to be detected. Kim wanted to laugh at that. Anyone could easily pick the men out of a crowd as security. Kim was even more astounded when the President walked around the long buffet and moved close to where she was standing.

Trying to ignore the man and avoid a confrontation, Kim instead began trying to make conversation with the guests who had come to the buffet. Something she was finding impossible, because each of them was trying instead to get the attention of the President.

A few minutes later, Kim jumped and turned to glare at the man standing next to her. The pinch she had felt on her backside could have only come from one place.

Ignoring the hate filled glare, the President's own face held a smug look as he turned away from Kim and began a speech to the crowd gathered in front of the buffet.
Not wanting to cause a commotion by confronting the man, Kim instead motioned

to the same man who had worked with her the night she'd heard the President's sons talking. Kim still couldn't remember the man's name. "Can you cover for a minute? I just need to run to the restroom."

Glad to be able to stand next to the President, the man nodded and moved up to take Rachel's spot. Relieved to get away, Rachel headed quickly to the restrooms in search of some peace.

Stepping inside, Kim was dismayed to see the room was full. Luckily, she found an empty stall and locked herself in. Feeling humiliated and irritated with herself for not confronting the President, Kim sat down on the toilet seat, but not to use the facilities. She was trying to collect herself. Taking deep breaths, Kim finally felt calm enough to pull out her phone and dial Brock's number.
He answered right away with a quick "What's going on?" before Kim jumped in. "That pompous jerk just pinched my ass, that's what's going on. Worse than that, I walked away without cussing him out or taking a swing at him."

A grin started to erupt before Brock forced it back. "You mean the President? I'm sorry Kim. The guy's a jerk, but you need to hold your temper and let it slide. I know that's easier said than done. You have to look at the bigger picture. Nothing can stop what we're planning tomorrow."

Kim sighed. "That doesn't help much. Damn it Brock. How can the guy think he can get away with doing something like that? He just stood there with a smug look on his face and acted like I wasn't worth looking at, only pinching."

Brock nodded. "I know it's frustrating. Let it go Kim. Listen, why don't you and Rachel meet Red and I after your shift? I noticed there was a bar next to the restaurant we were at earlier. I'll buy you a condolence drink."

A smile, Kim couldn't stop, replaced the scowl she'd been wearing. "Okay, but I'm ordering the most expensive drink in the bar."

Brock laughed. "Good for you. We'll see you and Rachel later. Hang in there."

Kim nodded. "Thanks Brock, I feel better just venting to you."

Hanging up the phone. Kim flushed the toilet she hadn't used and then took her time washing her hands before taking a deep breath and heading back to the buffet. Moving to the area, her spirits lifted, seeing the President had left. Probably off looking for another group he could boast to about how amazing he was.

Stepping behind the buffet, Kim thanked the other worker and resumed her shift. When it was finally over, Kim hurried to the dressing room to tell Rachel what had happened and about Brock's offer.

Although Rachel's shift was calmer than Kim's, she was happy to leave her temporary job and head to accept Brock's offer to buy drinks.

Heading into the bar was like stepping into a calm oasis compared with what they had left behind at Treasure Hill. Red and Brock stood and waved at the two women from a table sitting toward the back of the dimly lit bar. Smiling at the men, Rachel and Kim weaved around two pool tables before making their way over to the table and taking seats.

Running her hands through her hair, Kim shook her head. "I'm glad that shift is over. Can you believe the arrogance of the President? He grabbed my butt, then stood there like nothing happened. I feel awful I didn't call him out on the gesture. Any other day, I swear, he'd be missing a few teeth."

Brock smiled. "I'm just glad you held your temper. From what I've heard on the news, the guy does a lot worse things than that." Brock motioned at the waitress, but turned back to Kim. "Let's get you that drink. That should help to ease the pain a bit."

Nodding, Kim sighed. "You're right, and if all goes well, tomorrow I'll be laughing and the President will be in handcuffs."

Beside Kim, Rachel also nodded. "That's right and both of us can get back to our regular jobs as agents."
She laughed. "Then again, you never know where the next assignment will take you."

Pointing toward the pool tables, Red smiled. "How about we take our minds off that whole mess and play a game or two of pool?"

Giving Red a smirk, Rachel turned to Kim. "We can play, but I should warn you, this guy has a pool table in his house. Just don't make any bets on the outcome of the game. Red is a pool shark."

Kim laughed. "Getting beat at pool is better than getting pinched. I'd love to play. Let's get our drinks first though."

Fifteen minutes later, the drinks sat half-finished on the table, while the four agents stood not far away, holding pool sticks. Despite knowing they were at a disadvantage, Kim and Rachel had decided to partner up against the men.

Halfway through the second game, all four of the agents phones sounded. After exchanging puzzled looks, phones were quickly pulled from pockets.
The text messages the four received were identical and had the four exchanging high fives and fist bumps.

When they were finished, Kim was the first to express an opinion. "Looks like karma is real. I can't believe it. Knowing the warrant for that awful man's arrest is approved, makes that hurt over the pinch earlier a lot easier to take."

Brock smiled. "Sadly, it also means we're all going to have a big day tomorrow. I think we should finish this game, the drinks and head out. Hopefully we can all get a good night's rest."

The others agreed, although after the good news they'd just received, a bigger celebration seemed in order. If all went well though, they would only have to put it off for a short time.

Chapter 15

At Red's house and at Rachel's apartment the next morning, the agents were busy preparing early for what they knew was going to be an eventful day.

Brock and Red left Red's house a half an hour before Rachel and Kim left the apartment.

Meeting up in the FBI conference room, the four agents joined Travis, Aaron and Paul West, who had been working with Red and Brock patrolling the resort from the outside.

Sitting next to Travis, Aaron deferred to him as the head of the FBI in the area, even though he was actually the man's boss.

Travis stood. "Thanks to everyone for coming in early today. First thing I want to do is update everyone in the progress we've made and then walk you through how we are going to execute our plans for the President."

Looking around the table, Travis' gaze paused for a moment on each member of his team before retaking his seat. "The text you all received last night is accurate. We have been given an arrest warrant from not only a state judge, but also from a federal justice court."

Frowning, Kim raised her hand and interrupted Travis. "Can a sitting President be arrested? I mean, this guy has broken so many laws already it isn't funny."

It was Aaron who nodded his head and answered. "It has happened before. But, so far back in our history people don't remember. Grant was arrested for speeding. He was fined for the crime. With the charges we have, jail is a more appropriate action."

Travis nodded. "With collaborated testimony, both state and federal judges felt compelled to sign the warrants. We have testimony from Hal Ostrum swearing that the President was behind the bomb threats. The man apparently thought he could make the FBI look like they were negligent in their duties. He knew the bombs were fakes. The President hired Daniel Ortiz to pay

Cory Baxter to mail the letter to the FBI. Then he paid Ortiz to kill Cory Baxter." Shaking his head at the complicated plot, Travis continued. "According to not only Ostrum, but Jefferson Walcott, the President and his legal council Reuben Adelman linked up with a hypnotist years ago to plant subliminal messages into the minds of many of the President's hired flunkies."

Aaron nodded. "The guy was using others to do his dirty work for years. I think Adelman was more than likely the brains behind all of this, but the President, even when he was a business man, was more than happy to go along with the malicious and illegal acts. I don't know if we will ever discover the full extent of the crimes."

Silent a moment, Travis waited to see if anyone had more questions then he continued. "Ostrum used the subliminal suggestion and forced Ortiz to commit suicide. He says he didn't believe that Ortiz would find a way to kill himself. I believe Ostrum on that. The man acts sincere in his regret. Either way, whether he is sorry or just protecting himself, we have his testimony. We also have Jefferson Walcott stating he knew about the hypnosis used." Travis sighed. "I haven't agreed with many of the President's policies or the ways his team put them into effect, but I can't fathom what this President has done."

Sitting next to Kim, Brock frowned. "The Special Council knows a lot about the criminal activities and is still actively working the investigation. Will the President's arrest impede or even stop that altogether?"

Travis shrugged. "I can't answer that. There is no precedent for anything that is happening since a man like him was somehow elected to run our country. Although we can arrest him today, the President's lawyer will surely get him out on bail and try to get the charges dropped on a technicality. I have no doubt about that. The fact that we were able to get the warrant and make the arrest is what I am counting on to change congress' mind about covering for this guy."

A groan escaped before Kim could stop it. She was hoping the arrest later today would

take the President out of office and the
rebuilding of the country could begin. She
shook her head as all eyes focused on her.
"I'm sorry. I just expected this was the end
for the President. I guess I forgot how easily
the man has been able to create enough
chaos he hasn't had to answer for any of his
despicable and illegal acts."

Travis nodded. "We all can understand the
way you feel. One thing you can look
forward to is heading home after today.
Your part in the investigation will be over.
Maybe things will go better than we are
anticipating. Because of the past, we are all
thinking the worst. These charges are damn
serious and authenticated."
Shaking his head, Travis sighed. "Before we
worry about any of the repercussions the
President will face, we have to arrest him."
Sitting back in his chair, Travis turned to his
boss. "Aaron, it might be best if I let you
explain that."

Aaron nodded. "Thanks for bringing
everyone up to date."
Looking around the table, Aaron grinned.
"Now that we are all on the same page, let's

talk about today."

Aaron turned so he could address the two women at the table. "The two of you will be inside the resort and at the buffet today. From what we've been told, the buffet will be expanded for after the President's speech. We are waiting until after the speech to issue the warrant."

Staring at Aaron, Brock frowned. "Why wait? I thought we'd head over and grab the idiot before his big talk."

Aaron nodded. "We thought about that. In order to prevent a riot from his hard core followers, we decided against it. We plan on catching the President after he walks away from the podium and before he begins meetings with constituents."

Brock smiled. "Sounds like you thought this through better than I did."

The sound of Aaron's laugh filled the room. "Not the first time that's happened. Now, while Kim and Rachel are keeping an eye on things inside, the rest of us will be outside the resort watching for trouble. Travis will be in charge of issuing the

warrant. When he heads in, the rest of us follow. I should tell you we haven't notified the Secret Service about any of this. We felt it was better that way to avoid leaks. Does anyone have any more questions?"
When no one raised any queries, Aaron nodded. "Then, let's get the ball rolling."

Twenty minutes later, Travis, Aaron and part of their team were stationed outside the resort, while Kim and Rachel had changed into their uniforms and were helping set up the buffet. Their temporary boss, Rick Manor, knew Rachel and Kim were agents. He also knew something was happening judging by the curious looks he repeatedly gave the two women.

Trying to ignore Rick, Kim and Rachel, glad they were working together today, completed their job, while also scrutinizing the area for suspicious activity. For Kim, the investigation couldn't be over soon enough and her anxiety was high as she worried something would happen that would prevent her from heading home. She was certain once she returned, her life was going to be making a big modification. She was torn between sorrow at leaving the job she once loved and the happiness of knowing it was over. Pushing thoughts of the future from her mind, Kim focused her attention on the present. Although Kim didn't actually know any of the other workers at the resort, the faces had become familiar to her. The brown eyes narrowed and a frown creased her forehead as Kim watched a man who looked to be in his thirties carrying a large bag. Kim nudged Rachel's elbow and leaned toward her, whispering. "Rachel, who's that guy? I don't remember seeing him before."

Looking in the direction of Kim's stare, Rachel also frowned. "I don't know him either. Hang on a minute, I'll go ask Rick."

Continuing to watch the man, Kim anxiously waited for Rachel's return. Although Rachel was only gone a few minutes, Kim felt like time was standing still. Concentrating on the stranger, who was now just standing and holding his bag, Kim was startled when Rachel stepped over to her and began speaking quietly.

"Rick said that guy is a replacement worker. He's just filling in for today. One of the regulars has the flu. He sent this guy in his place knowing how busy the resort would be with the President here."

Kim shook her head. "Something's not right. I haven't seen that guy do any work. He's been standing over there holding that bag since I first noticed him."
Reaching in her pocket, Kim pulled out her phone and hit the speed dial for Brock.

Outside, Brock felt his phone vibrate in his back pocket and grabbed it out quickly, knowing who the call had to be from. A quick glance at the caller ID proved him right. "What's going on Kim?"

Not wasting time with a greeting, Kim sighed. "I think we've got a problem. I'm sure the guy I'm watching shouldn't be here. He breeched security by replacing another worker for the day. I'm going to confront him, but wanted to give you a description in case he runs. Six foot tall, around two hundred pounds. The guys' dark hair is partially covered in one of the Presidents' red, Make American Great Again hats. He has on black pants and like the rest of us a cheap looking gold shirt. I'm handing my phone to Rachel, she can keep you updated while I confront this guy."

Brock frowned. "Maybe you should wait for more backup Kim. With this crowd, it will take me at least ten minutes to get in there."

Kim shook her head. "Rachel's here, we'll be fine."
Without waiting for a response, Kim handed the phone to Rachel and began moving toward the man. Before she reached him, Kim yelled out. "Hey, can I talk to you a minute?"

Staring at the man as he looked over at her, Kim could see fear in the dark eyes. Taking a firmer grip on the bag he carried, the man started to turn away. Knowing he was going to bolt, Kim reached down and pulled her gun from its' ankle holster. She straightened up and lifted the gun, pointing the barrel at the man. "FBI, hold it right there."

Behind Kim, Rachel also reached for her pistol, while talking to Brock. "He's going to make a run for it."

Outside, Brock turned to Red who was standing a few feet away. "We got a problem. I need to get in there. Kim and Rachel are…"

Before Brock finished his statement, a loud explosion was followed by a rush of air. Brock felt himself being lifted off his feet and thrown backwards. To him, it felt like an invisible giant had picked him up and thrown him. Landing hard on the ground on his back, Brock lifted his hands to cover his face as debris rained down. Struggling to sit up, Brock looked to his left and saw Red lying under a pile of rubble. Instead of standing, Brock crawled to Red. Reaching him, Brock grabbed the agents' shoulder. "Red, are you okay? Can you move?"

The green eyes fluttered a few times before opening wide. "I'm okay. Just got the wind knocked out of me. Damn, what happened?"

Brock shook his head. "A bomb, someone just blew up the resort."
The green eyes darkened with concern. "Kim and Rachel. Oh hell. I have to find them."
As Brock stood, Red also struggled to his feet. The two men stared in shock at the

scene in front of them. The hotel was nothing but a pile of rubble. The two could already see people digging in the wreckage. The screams, neither had noticed before, now seemed to fill the air.

Both men began running toward the catastrophe, tripping over stone, wood and other debris as they ran.

Seeing Aaron ahead of them pulling away boards from a pile, Brock pointed. "There's Aaron, c'mon, let's go help. We have to find Kim, Rachel and the others."

The two began rushing toward Aaron as the sound of sirens slit like a knife through the air. Even before the two reached Aaron and began digging, they knew it was too late. No one inside the building or within twenty feet of the place could have survived the bombing.

Desperately digging and throwing the rubble as they did, it was also evident none of the men was ready to give up the search for their fellow agents who were also their friends.

Chapter 16

Back in Washington D.C., Brock was sitting at his desk when he heard a knock on the door. Since the explosion at Treasure Hill, Brock had been given a temporary desk job. Brock had never had to do anything harder than explaining what had happened to Kim's husband Blake. After the heart wrenching ordeal of attending Kim's funeral, Brock was glad for the new position. However, like Kim had done, Brock was reconsidering his decision to be an agent. He'd known fellow agents who had died in service, but the death of his temporary partner was like an acid eating at him from the inside out.

Brock had been through a lot in his time as an agent, but nothing had bothered him more than meeting with Blake Mackey to try and explain why Kim had died.

Two weeks had passed since the explosion and Brock found he couldn't think of anything but that day. The sound of the

explosion still rang in his mind, as did the last words he had heard from Kim. She had said 'Rachel's here, we'll be fine'.
Thinking of those words, Brock shook his head and wondered if anything would ever be fine again. Trying to ignore the nagging thoughts, Brock focused his attention on his closed door where the earlier sound had come from. "C'mon in."

Pushing the door opened, Aaron stepped inside and closed the door behind him. "I think it's time for you to take on an assignment."

Brock shook his head as Aaron stepped over and took a seat across from him. "I'm not ready Aaron. Until I am, I'm of no use to you. I would only hinder an investigation and endanger others."

Brock was surprised to see a crooked grin on Aaron's face. Brock's boss shook his head. "I think this case will make you change your mind."

Despite his misgivings, Brock's curiosity had him staring at Aaron. "What makes you think that?"

Reaching in his pocket, Aaron pulled out a cassette tape. "I think you should listen to this. The recording will explain everything much better than I can."

Frowning, Brock opened a drawer in his desk and pulled out an antique looking, battery operated, cassette player. He placed it on the desk.

Pulling the machine to him, Aaron put in the tape and pressed play. The sound of a woman's voice could be heard amid some crackling and static because of the antiquated mode of recording Aaron had used.

"Are you sure everything is set up? What if the explosion isn't big enough."

A man's voice, not much deeper than the woman's answered. "Everything's been taken care of. No one in the resort is going to survive. We'll finally be rid of not only your father, but those sick brothers of yours."

A short break was followed by the man speaking again. "You're not going to back out are you? Think about everything that has been done to you over the years."

The sound of a woman's light laughter could be heard before she spoke. "I want this more than anything in the world. Are you sure the bombing can't be traced back to us?"

Now the man laughed. "Don't I always cover our backs?"

Reaching forward, Aaron hit the stop button. "There's a bit more, but you get the idea."

Green eyes wide, Brock shook his head. "Is that who I think it was?"

Aaron nodded. "The President's daughter and son-in-law. Before the President headed to Treasure Hill, I was looking into why those two, for the most part, avoided the President's big ceremonies. I was even more focused after Kim overheard the President's sons talking."

Brock winced at the sound of his dead partner's name, but focused on what Aaron was saying.

"I knew the two were headed to the resort in Colorado. I arranged for the recording to be set up. I didn't get the finalized tapes until a week ago. Then, I had to get the warrants in order before I decided it was time to bring it all to you. I thought you'd be the perfect person to come with me and make this arrest."

Brock smiled. "Thanks Aaron. When do we go?"

I hope you enjoyed the story. The events depicted, although they may sound close to reality, are fiction. I love conspiracies and hope you found this one worth a bit of your time.

I have to thank my family and friends for their support as I continue writing. Special thanks and a shout out to my husband who has to live with such a crazy lady and puts up with me despite that condition.

Although I have been handed a few challenges in my health lately, it is family, friends and the wonderful readers of my books that have helped me find innovative ways to continue in this journey of being an author, that I love.
Without you, none of my dreams could have come true.

I hope to continue writing and hope you will look for all of my books on Amazon and Barnes and Noble. I hope you will head

over, type in P.S. Winn under books and
join me in all the journeys.
52 down and counting. ☺